"BANKING LAWS

&

E-BANKING

Dr. DEVENDRA SINGH

M.Com,M.B.A, LL.B., Ph.D.

PREFACE

The introduction of electronic banking into the banking sector is to bring customer satisfaction thereby enhancing the bank's' profitability. Compared to ordinary banking system electronic banking is providing the competitive advantage by lowering the cost and providing best satisfaction of customer needs. But unless this technology curtails certain risk that comes along with it, there would not be the requisite increase in customer satisfaction over the traditional bank branches and customer may perceive it as the same as different branches rather than a new means of delivery channels. The benefit of e-banking from customer point of view is convenience to access account 24/7, that is, access is not limited to banking operation hours and available around the clock, wherever the customer's located on the other side people are generally shy of use of these services because of the perceived risk of failure, complexity and security.

Therefore for the smooth amalgamation of e-banking into the traditional banking services, certain technological variations as well as legal amendments were made to the present banking laws in India. The impacts of these amendments are quite apparent and would be dealt with in the dissertation. Internet banking is a popular and convenient method of doing online banking transactions. We have no dedicated Internet banking laws in India but the Reserve Bank of India (RBI) has issued some guidelines in this regard. However, Internet banking guidelines in India by RBI are not sufficient to make the banks follow robust and required cyber security procedures. This means that Internet banking risks in India are high and even RBI acknowledged risks of e-banking in India. Despite this position, banks in India are ignoring the cyber security due diligence requirements prescribed by RBI. The online banking risks in India have increased tremendously due to this position. The legal issues of Internet banking in India must be taken more seriously by all stakeholders especially the Indian banks. However, better results cannot be achieved till cyber security requirements made mandatory on the part of Indian banks.

I have emphasized to maintain the basic essence of the book in presenting the subject clear, articulate manner and include updates.

The book is designed for individual who have Law, banking students & professional or equivalent to a bachelor's degree in management and banking competitive exams.

I would like to thanks to my family members, Mrs. Swati C., Mrs. Krishna D., Mr. C.L. Singh, and Master Divyansh for their endurance through the years that I devoted in writing this book. Special thanks to Ms.Rashi, who have helped me in collecting & organizing the manuscript, formatting, chart & tables in this book.

ORGANISATION OF BOOK

The whole book is divided in to seven chapters-

Chapter one shall address the Overview & History , development in Banking Law , Growth of Banking in India and adoption of E-Banking technology , Various Forms of E-banking .

Chapter two is about Nature, Concept, Scope of E-Banking System and Laws in the Indian banking system. This chapter covers Law of Banking, E-banking in India, Adaptation of E-banking in India and Services, facilities through E-banking in detail.

Chapter three elaborates the Legal Aspects of E-Banking operations in India such as Indian Experience of E-banking, Obligations of Banks and E-Banking ,Guidelines by RBI to Banks Regarding E-Banking, Legal Risks and Compliances, Strategic risk, Reputation Risk and Initiatives by Government to Develop E-Banking.

Chapter four states the Laws Relating to E-banking and high lights the law & provisions related with banks such as Information Technology Act, 2000, First Case Convicted under Information Technology Act 2000 of India, Reserve Bank of India Act, 1934, Banking Regulation Act, 1949,Negotiable Instruments Act, 1881 and Other Relevant Acts such as Bankers Books Evidence Act, 1891, Prevention of Money Laundering Act, 2002, Indian Contract Act, 1872, Indian Penal Code, 1860,

Indian Evidence Act, 1872 and Consumer Protection Act, 1986.

Chapter five focuses on the Problems Faced by E-Banking System in India and covers topic in detail like Types of Frauds- Electronic Fraud, Identity Fraud, Spyware and Adware, Wire Fraud, Impersonation or Identity Theft, Credit Card Fraud, Booster Cheques, Duplication or Skimming of Card Information, Money Laundering, E-banking Frauds and overall scenario of E-Banking Frauds in India.

Chapter six focuses on the Comparative E-banking Laws of Other Countries like United States of America, United Kingdom and France.

Chapter Seven is about the Suggestion for Improving E-banking System in India.

The Objectives of book is-

To identify various e-banking services/products adopted by Indian banks.

To study and analyze the progress made by Indian banking industry in adoption of technology.

To study the challenges faced by Indian banks in adoption of technology and make recommendations to tackle these challenges.

To Study existing banking laws in relation with E-Banking Services.

To analyze the implication of E-Banking Laws on the Banking system.

To recommend improvements in the existing E-Banking Laws and system.

Table of Contents

15

17

TABLE OF CASES

CASES
1-Deepak Prem Manwani Case,(India's First ATM Card Fraud)
2-Vimal Chandra Grover v. Bank of India,AIR 2000 SC 2181, 2002(2) BLJR 1604
3-Tournier v. National Provincial & Union Bank of England,(1934) KB, 461
4-Sanjay Kumar Kedia v. Narcotic,Control Bureau & Anr,Appeal (clr.) 1659 of 2007
State of Tamil Nadu v. Suhas Katti
5-Syed Asifuddin & Ors v. State of Andhra Pradesh & Ors,2006(1) ALD Cri 96, 2005 Cri LJ 4314
6-P. Padmanabh v. Syndicate Bank LTD. *AIR 2008 Kant 42, 2008(1) Kar LJ 153*

LIST OF ABBREVIATIONS

AIR	ALL INDIA REPORT
GOVT.	GOVERNMENT
ART.	ARTICLE
ATM	AUTOMATED TELLER MACHINE
EFT	ELECTRONIC FUNDS TRANSFER
IPC	INDIAN PENAL CODE
SC	SUPREME COURT
IT	INFORMATION TECHNOLOGY
MICR	MAGNETIC INKS CHARACTER
V	VERSUS
ETS	ELECTRONIC

	TRANSACTIONAL SYSTEM
FDIC	FEDERAL DEPOSIT INSURANCE CORPORATION
NEFT	NATIONAL ELECTRONIC FUNDS TRANSFER
CVV	CARD VERIFICATION VALUE
IRC	INTERNET RELAY CHAT
KYC	KNOW YOUR CUSTOMER
C LR	CRIME LAW REPORT
CRILJ	CRIME LAW JOURNAL
CRPC	CRIMINAL PROCEDURE CODE
WOS	WHOLLY OWNED SUBSIDIARY
ECS	ELECTRONIC CLEARING SERVICE

CHAPTER I:
INTRODUCTION

1.1 Overview

A bank is a financial institution that provides banking and other financial services to their customers. A bank is generally understood as an institution which provides fundamental banking services such as accepting deposits and providing loans. There are also nonbanking institutions that provide certain banking services without meeting the legal definition of a bank. Banks are a subset of the financial services industry. A banking system also referred as a system provided by the bank which offers cash management services for customers, reporting the transactions of their accounts and portfolios, throughout the day. The banking system in India should not only be hassle free but it should be able to meet the new challenges posed by the technology and any other external and internal factors. For the past three decades, India's banking system has several outstanding achievements to its credit.

The Banks are the main participants of the financial system in India. The Banking sector offers several facilities and opportunities to their customers. The entire bank's safeguards the money and valuables and provide loans, credit, and payment services, such as checking accounts, money orders, and cashier's cheques. The banks also offer investment and insurance products. As a variety of models for cooperation and integration among finance industries have emerged, some of the traditional distinctions between banks, insurance companies, and securities firms have diminished. In spite of these changes, banks continue to maintain and perform their primary role—accepting deposits and lending funds from these deposits.[1]

E-banking these days is the one of the quickest growing developments in Indian banking and is poised to take the banking sector a notch better. No

[1] Varying Impacts of Electronic Banking on the Banking Industry, *available at:* http://www.icommercecentral.com/open-access/varying-impacts-of-electronic-banking-on-the-banking-industry.php?aid=59264 (visited on October 15, 2017)

extra falling in line in banks, no extra waiting lots of hours inside the financial institution, no greater days and weeks of ready. All can be accomplished with one card, on gadget. It's clean, it really works, and most importantly, humans adore it. But nonetheless, some humans are having a tough time using this form of era, often people who are used to do matters the antique traditional way.

With using advertising, people are actually motivated to apply E-banking because again, it gets rid of the problem encountered whilst the usage of the old process of banking. The development of digital banking or usually known as e-banking, began with the usage of automatic teller machines (ATMs) and has included telephone banking, direct invoice fee, electronic fund transfer, online banking and other digital transactions for plenty human beings, they accept as true with that the e-banking will go to the path of cellular banking also, some human beings believe that online banking may be the maximum popular technique in the future. In order for users/customers to apply their bank's online offerings, they need to have a personal laptop and a web connection. Additionally, their private computer systems might be their assistant who will help them in their transactions and offerings. Examples of those transactions are paying payments, obtaining data about bills and loans, and so forth. E-Banking (an abbreviation for electronic banking) is an umbrella time period for the system by way of which a patron might also carry out banking transactions electronically without journeying a brick-and-mortar institution. In simple terms, it does now not contain any bodily alternate of money, but it's all done electronically, from one account to every other, the use of the net. From a personal laptop, you may access bank account facts, and carry out many banking features, like transferring cash, creating a mortgage price. Electronic banking, also called digital fund transfer (EFT), makes use of laptop and electronic technology as an alternative for tests and different paper transactions. In simple words, the structures that enable monetary organization customers, people or companies, to get admission to accounts, transact commercial enterprise, or gain facts on monetary services and products via a public or private network, including the internet i.e. pc, ATM, on line banking, and many others . It way any person with a personal laptop and a browser can get related to his bank -s internet site to carry out any of the digital banking features. In net banking device the financial institution has a centralized database that is internet-enabled. All the offerings that the financial institution has authorized on the net are displayed in menu. Any service may be selected and similarly interaction is dictated by using the nature of carrier.

The traditional branch version of bank is now giving place to an opportunity transport channels with ATM community. As soon as the branch workplaces of financial institution are interconnected via terrestrial or satellite TV for pc links, there could be no bodily identification for any branch. It would a without borders entity permitting each time, anywhere and anyways banking.

Need of Banks

Before the establishment of banks, the financial activities were handled by money lenders and individuals. At that time the interest rates were very high. Again there were no security of public savings and no uniformity regarding loans. So as to overcome such problems the organized banking sector was established, which was fully regulated by the government. The organized banking sector works within the financial system to provide loans, accept deposits and provide other services to their customers. The following functions of the bank explain the need of the bank and its importance[2]:

• To provide the security to the savings of customers.

2 The Importance of E-banking in Business, *available at:* http://http://smallbusiness.chron.com/importance-ebanking-business-26188.html
(Visited on October 15, 2017)

• To control the supply of money and credit

• To encourage public confidence in the working of the financial system, increase savings speedily and efficiently.

• To avoid focus of financial powers in the hands of a few individuals and institutions.

• To set equal norms and conditions (i.e. rate of interest, period of lending etc) to all types of customers.

E-banking these days is the one of the quickest growing developments in Indian banking and is poised to take the banking sector a notch better. No extra falling in line in banks, no extra waiting lots of hours inside the financial institution, no greater days and weeks of ready. All can be accomplished with one card, on gadget. It's clean, it really works, and most importantly, humans adore it but nonetheless, some humans are having a tough time using this form of era, often people who are used to do matters the antique traditional way.

With using advertising, people are actually motivated to apply E-banking because again, it gets rid of the problem encountered whilst the usage of the old process of banking. The development of digital banking or usually known as e-banking, began with the usage of automatic teller machines (ATMs) and has included telephone banking, direct invoice fee ,electronic fund transfer, online banking and other digital transactions for plenty human beings, they accept as true with that the e-banking will go to the path of cellular banking. Also, some human beings believe that online banking may be the maximum popular technique in the future. In order for users/customers to apply their bank's online offerings, they need to have a personal laptop and a web connection. Additionally, their private computer systems might be their assistant who will help them in their transactions and offerings. Examples of those transactions are paying payments, obtaining data about bills and loans, and so forth. E-Banking (an abbreviation for electronic banking) is an umbrella time period for the system by way of which a patron might also carry out banking transactions electronically without journeying a brick-and-mortar institution. In simple terms, it does now not contain any bodily alternate of money, but it's all done electronically, from one account to every other, the use of the net. From a personal laptop, you may access bank account facts, and carry out many banking features, like transferring cash, creating a mortgage price. Electronic banking, also called digital fund transfer (EFT), makes use of laptop and electronic technology as an alternative for tests and different paper transactions. In simple words, the structures that enable monetary organization customers, people or companies, to get admission to accounts, transact commercial enterprise, or gain facts on monetary services and products via a public or private network, including the internet i.e. pc, ATM, on line banking, and many others . It way any person with a personal laptop and a browser can get related to his bank -s internet site to carry out any of the digital banking features. In net banking device the financial institution has a centralized database that is internet-enabled. All the offerings that the financial institution has authorized on the net are displayed in menu. Any service may be selected and similarly interaction is dictated by using the nature of carrier.

The traditional branch version of bank is now giving place to an opportunity transport channels with ATM community. As soon as the branch workplaces of financial institution are interconnected via terrestrial or satellite TV for pc links, there could be no bodily identification for any branch. It would a without borders entity permitting each time, anywhere and anyways banking.[3]

---

[3] Why we need banks, *available at:* http://hbr.org/2010/06/why-we-need-banks
(Visited on October 15, 2017)

1.2 History and Development in Banking Law

HISTORY OF BANKING

In historical India there may be evidence of loans from the Vedic length (beginning 1750 BC). Later the duration of the Maurya dynasty (321 to 185 BC), an instrument known as adesha become in exercise, which become an order on a banker craving him to pay the cash of the word to a 3rd person, which resembles to the meaning of a invoice of change as we recognize it these days. Throughout the Buddhist length, there was giant use of those devices. Merchants in big towns gave letters of credit to one another .Banking in India in the modern sense originated in the last decades of the 18th century. Among the first banks were the Bank of Hindustan, which was established in 1770 and liquidated in 1829-32; and the General financial institution, established in 1786 but failed in 1791.The biggest bank and the oldest nonetheless in lifestyles, is the kingdom bank of India. It originated

33

because the financial institution of Calcutta in June 1806. In 1809, it changes into renamed because the financial institution of Bengal. This becomes one of the three banks funded through a presidency authorities; the opposite had been the financial institution of Bombay and the financial institution of Madras. The 3 banks have been merged in 1921 to form the Imperial financial institution of India, which after India's independence, have become the state financial institution of India in 1955. for decades the presidency banks had represented as quasi-crucial banks, as did their successors, till the Reserve financial institution of India changed into hooked up in 1935, underneath the Reserve financial institution of India Act, 1934.[45]

In 1960, the kingdoms financial institution of India changed into given manage of eight nation-associated

[4]History of Indian Banking - An Overview, *available at:*http://shodhganga.inflibnet.ac.in/bitstream/10603/11587/10/10_chapter%203.pdf
(Visited on October 15, 2017)
[5]*ibid*

banks beneath the country bank of India (Subsidiary Banks) Act, 1959. Those are now referred to as its accomplice banks. In 1969 the Indian authorities nationalized 14 principal private banks. In 1980, 6 more private banks were nationalized. These nationalized banks are the majority of lenders in the Indian economic system. They dominate the banking quarter due to their massive size and sizeable networks.

The Indian banking sector is broadly classified into scheduled banks and non-scheduled banks. The scheduled banks are those which are included under the 2nd Schedule of the Reserve Bank of India Act, 1934. The scheduled banks are further classified into: nationalized banks; State Bank of India and its associates; Regional Rural Banks (RRBs); foreign banks; and other Indian private sector banks. The term commercial banks refer to both scheduled and nonscheduled commercial banks which are regulated under the Banking Regulation Act, 1949.

Normally banking in India is fairly mature in phrases of deliver, product range and reach-despite the fact that attain in rural India and to the negative nonetheless stays a project. The authorities had developed initiatives to cope with this through the nation bank of India expanding its branch network and via the countrywide financial institution for Agriculture and Rural development with centers like microfinance.

Ancient India

The Vedas (2000-1400 BCE) are earliest Indian texts to mention the concept of usury. The word Kusidin is translated as usurer. The Sutras (700-100 BCE) and the Jatakas (600-400 BCE) also mention usury. Also, during this period, texts began to condemn usury. Vasishtha forbade Brahmin and Kshatriya varnas from participating in usury. By 2nd century CE, usury seems to have become more acceptable. The Manusmriti considers usury an acceptable means of acquiring wealth or leading a livelihood. It also considers money lending above a certain rate, different ceiling rates for different caste, and a grave sin.

The Jatakas also mention the existence of loan deeds. These were called rnapatra or rnapanna. The Dharmashastras also supported the use of loan deeds. Kautilya has also mentioned the usage of loan deeds. Loans deeds were also called rnalekhaya.

Later during the Mauryan period (321-185 BCE), an instrument called adesha was in use, which was an order on a banker directing him to pay the sum on the note to a third person, which corresponds to the definition of a modern bill of exchange. The considerable use of these instruments has been recorded. In large towns, merchants also gave letters of credit to one another.

Medieval period

The use of loan deeds continued into the Mughal era and was called dastawez. Two types of loans deeds have been recorded. The dastawez-eindultalab was payable on demand and dastawez-e-miadi was payable after a stipulated time. The use of payment orders by royal treasuries, called barattes, has been also noted. There are also accounts of Indian bankers using issuing bills of exchange on foreign countries. The evolution of hundis, a type of credit mechanism, also occurred during this period and they continue to be in use today.

Colonial era

During the period of British rule merchants established the Union Bank of Calcutta in 1869, first as a private joint stock association, the partnership. Its proprietors were the owners of the earlier Commercial Bank and the Calcutta Bank, who by mutual consent created Union Bank to replace these two banks. In 1840 it established an agency at Singapore, and closed the one at Mirzapore that it had opened in the previous year. Also in 1840 the Bank revealed that it had been the subject of a fraud by the bank's accountant. Union Bank was incorporated in 1845 but failed in 1848, having been insolvent for some time and having used new money from depositors to pay its dividends.

The Allahabad Bank, established in 1865 and still functioning today, is the oldest Joint Stock bank in India; it was not the first though. That honour belongs to the Bank of Upper India, which was established in 1863, and which survived until 1913, when it failed, with some of its assets and liabilities being shifted to the Alliance Bank of Shimla.

Foreign banks too started to appear, particularly in Calcutta, in the 1860s. The Compote d'Escompte de Paris opened a branch in Calcutta in 1860, and another in Bombay in 1862; branches in Madras and Pondicherry, then a French possession, followed. HSBC established itself in Bengal in 1869. Calcutta was the most active trading port in India, mainly due to the trade of the British Empire, and so became a banking centre.

The first entirely Indian joint stock bank was the Oudh Commercial Bank, established in 1881 in Faizabad. It failed in 1958. The following was the Punjab National Bank, established in Lahore in 1894, which has survived to the present and is now one of the leading banks in India.

Around the turn of the 20th Century, the Indian economy was passing through a relative period of stability. Around five decades had elapsed since the Indian rebellion, and the social, industrial and other infrastructure had improved. Indians had established small banks, most of which served particular ethnic and religious communities.

The presidency banks dominated banking in India but there were also some exchange banks and a number of Indian joint stock banks. All these banks operated in different segments of the economy. The exchange banks, mostly owned by Europeans, concentrated on financing foreign trade. Indian joint stock banks were generally undercapitalized and lacked the experience and maturity to compete with the presidency and exchange banks. This segmentation let Lord Curzon to observe, "In respect of banking it seems we are behind the times. We are like some old fashioned sailing ship, divided by solid wooden bulkheads into separate and cumbersome compartments."

The period between 1906 and 1911, saw the establishment of banks inspired by the Swadeshi movement. The Swadeshi movement inspired local businessmen and political figures to found banks of and for the Indian community. A number of banks established then have survived to the present such as The South Indian Bank, Bank of India, Corporation Bank, Indian Bank, Bank of Baroda, Canara Bank and Central Bank of India.

The fervour of Swadeshi movement lead to establishing of many private banks in Dakshina Kannada and Udupi district which were unified earlier and known by the name South Canara (South Kanara) district. Four nationalized banks started in this district and also a leading private sector bank. Hence undivided Dakshina Kannada district is known as "Cradle of Indian Banking".

During the First World War (1914–1918) through the end of the Second World War (1939–1945), and two years thereafter until the independence of India were challenging for Indian banking. The years of the First World War were turbulent, and it took its toll with banks simply collapsing despite the Indian economy gaining indirect boost due to war-related economic activities. At least 94 banks in India failed between 1913 and 1918 as indicated in the following table:

Post-Independence period

The partition of India in 1947 adversely impacted the economies of Punjab and West Bengal, paralyzing banking activities for months. India's independence marked the end of a regime of the Laissez-faire for the Indian banking. The Government of India initiated measures to play an active role in the economic life of the

42

nation, and the Industrial Policy Resolution adopted by the government in 1948 envisaged a mixed economy. This resulted into greater involvement of the state in different segments of the economy including banking and finance. The major steps to regulate banking included.

The Reserve Bank of India, India's central banking authority, was established in April 1935, but was nationalized on 1 January 1949 under the terms of the Reserve Bank of India (Transfer to Public Ownership) Act, 1948 (RBI, 2005b).

In 1949, the Banking Regulation Act was enacted which empowered the Reserve Bank of India (RBI) "to regulate, control, and inspect the banks in India".

The Banking Regulation Act also provided that no new bank or branch of an existing bank could be opened without a license from the RBI, and no two banks could have common directors.[6]

Nationalization in the 1960s

Despite the provisions, control and regulations of the Reserve Bank of India, banks in India except the State Bank of India (SBI), continued to be owned and operated by private persons. By the 1960s, the Indian banking industry had become an important tool to facilitate the development of the Indian economy. At the same time, it had emerged as a large employer, and a debate had ensued about the nationalization of the banking industry. Indira Gandhi, the then Prime Minister of India, expressed the intention of the Government of India in the annual conference of the All India Congress Meeting in a paper entitled "Stray thoughts on Bank Nationalization."The meeting received the paper with enthusiasm.

---

[6] Indian Banking History, *available at: http://www.jagranjosh.com/articles/history-of-indian-banking-system-an-overview-1495540364-1* (Visited on October 19, 2017)

Thereafter, her move was swift and sudden. The Government of India issued an ordinance ('Banking Companies (Acquisition and Transfer of Undertakings) Ordinance, 1969') and nationalized the 14 largest commercial banks with effect from the midnight of 19 July 1969. These banks contained 85 percent of bank deposits in the country. Jayaprakash Narayan, a national leader of India, described the step as a "masterstroke of political sagacity." Within two weeks of the issue of the ordinance, the Parliament passed the Banking Companies (Acquisition and Transfer of Undertaking) Bill, and it received the presidential approval on 9 August 1969.

A second dose of nationalization of 6 more commercial banks followed in 1980.The specified reason for the nationalization was to give the government more control of credit delivery. With the second dose of nationalization, the Government of India controlled around 91% of the banking business of India. Later on, in the year 1993, the government merged

New Bank of India with Punjab National Bank. It was the only merger between nationalized banks and resulted in the reduction of the number of nationalized banks from 20 to 19. After this, until the 1990s, the nationalized banks grew at a pace of around 4%, closer to the average growth rate of the Indian economy.

Liberalization in the 1990s

In the early 1990s, the then government embarked on a policy of liberalization, licensing a small number of private banks. These came to be known as New Generation tech-savvy banks, and included Global Trust Bank (the first of such new generation banks to be set up), which later amalgamated with Oriental Bank of Commerce, UTI Bank (since renamed Axis Bank), ICICI Bank and HDFC Bank. This move, along with the rapid growth in the economy of India, revitalized the banking sector in India, which has seen rapid growth with strong contribution from all the three sectors of banks, namely, government banks, private banks and foreign banks.

The next stage for the Indian banking has been set up with the proposed relaxation in the norms for foreign direct investment, where all foreign investors in banks may be given voting rights which could exceed the present cap of 10% at present. It has gone up to 74% with some restrictions.

The new policy shook the Banking sector in India completely. Bankers, till this time, were used to the 4–6–4 method (borrow at 4%; lend at 6%; go home at 4) of functioning. The new wave ushered in a modern outlook and tech-savvy methods of working for traditional banks. All this led to the retail boom in India. People demanded more from their banks and received more.[7]

Current period

The Indian banking sector is broadly classified into scheduled banks and

---

[7] *ibid*

non-scheduled banks. All banks which are included in the Second Schedule to the Reserve Bank of India Act, 1934 are Scheduled Banks. These banks comprise Scheduled Commercial Banks and Scheduled Co-operative Banks. Scheduled Co-operative Banks consist of Scheduled State Co-operative Banks and Scheduled Urban Cooperative Banks. Scheduled Commercial Banks in India are categorized into five different groups according to their ownership and/or nature of operation:

State Bank of India and its Associates

Nationalized Banks

Private Sector Banks

Foreign Banks

Regional Rural Banks.

In the bank group-wise classification, IDBI Bank Ltd. is included in Nationalized Banks.

1.3 Growth of Banking in India

By 2010, banking in India was generally fairly mature in terms of supply, product range and reach-even though reach in rural India still remains a challenge for the private sector and foreign banks. In terms of quality of assets and capital adequacy, Indian banks are considered to have clean, strong and transparent balance sheets relative to other banks in comparable economies in its region. The Reserve Bank of India is an autonomous body, with minimal pressure from the government.

With the growth in the Indian economy expected to be strong for quite some time-especially in its services sector-the demand for banking services, especially retail banking, mortgages and investment services are expected to be strong. One may also expect M&A, takeovers, and asset sales.

In March 2006, the Reserve Bank of India allowed Warburg Pincus to increase its stake in Kotak Mahindra Bank (a private sector bank) to 10%. This is the first time an investor has been allowed to hold more than 5% in a private sector bank since the RBI announced norms in 2005 that any stake exceeding 5% in the private sector banks would need to be vetted by them.

In recent years critics have charged that the non-government owned banks are too aggressive in their loan recovery efforts in connexion with housing, vehicle and personal loans. There are press reports that the bank's' loan recovery efforts have driven defaulting borrowers to suicide.

By 2013 the Indian Banking Industry employed 1,175,149 employees and had a total of 109,811 branches in India and 171 branches abroad and manages an aggregate deposit of ☐67504.54 billion (US$1.0 trillion or €910 billion) and bank credit of ☐52604.59 billion (US$780 billion or €710 billion). The net profit of the banks operating in India was ☐1027.51 billion (US$15 billion or €14 billion) against a turnover of ☐9148.59 billion (US$140 billion or

€120 billion) for the financial year 2012-13.[8]

PradhanMantri Jan - Dhan Yojana (Accounts Opened As on 12.01.2015).[9]

PradhanMantri Jan Dhan Yojana is a scheme for comprehensive economic inclusion launched with the aid of the top Minister of India, NarendraModi, in 2014. Run by department of monetary offerings, Ministry of Finance, at the inauguration day, 1.5 Crore (15 million) financial institution money owed were opened underneath this scheme by means of 15 July 2015, 16.92 crore accounts have been opened, with around ☐20288.37 crore (US$three.zero billion) have been deposited underneath the scheme, which additionally has an option for commencing new bank bills with 0 balance.

---

[8]Growth of Banking and Development in India
http://theviewspaper.net/growth-of-banking-and-development-in-india/
available at: (Visited on October 17, 2017)
[9]Pradhan Mantri Jan Dhan Yojana (PMJDY) *available at:*
https://pmjdy.gov.in/ (Visited on October 17, 2017)

Banking codes and standards

The Banking Codes and requirements Board of India is an independent and independent banking industry which reveal all available banks in India whilst turning in services to customers. To improve the great of banking offerings in India SS Tarapore (former deputy governor of RBI) came up with the idea to form a committee.

1.4 Adoption of E-banking technology

The IT revolution has had a super effect at the Indian banking gadget. Using computer systems has caused the advent of online banking in India. The usage of computer systems in the banking region in India has accelerated many folds after the financial liberalization of 1991 as the country's banking zone has been uncovered to the arena's market. Indian banks were locating it tough to compete with the international banks in terms of customer support, without the usage of statistics generation.

In 1984 changed into fashioned the Committee on Mechanization in the Banking enterprise (1984) whose chairman was Dr. C Rangarajan, Deputy Governor, Reserve financial institution of India. The major recommendations of this committee had been introducing MICR technology in all the banks inside the metropolises in India. This furnished for using standardized cheque bureaucracy and encoders.

In 1988, the RBI installation the Committee on Computerization in Banks (1988) headed by Dr. C Rangarajan. It emphasized that agreement operation should be computerized in the clearing houses of RBI in Bhubaneshwar, Guwahati, Jaipur, Patna and Thiruvananthapuram. It in addition said that there ought to be countrywide Clearing of inter-city cheques at Kolkata, Mumbai, Delhi, Chennai and MICR ought to be made operational. It also focused on computerization of branches and increasing connectivity among branches via computer systems. It additionally suggested modalities for enforcing online banking. The committee submitted its reports in 1989 and computerization commenced from 1993 with the agreement between IBA and financial institution employees' associations.[10]

In 1994, the Committee on technology issues referring to charge systems, Cheque Clearing and Securities agreement inside the Banking enterprise (1994) was installation beneath Chairman W S Saraf. It emphasized electronic funds switch (EFT) system, with the BANKNET communications network as its provider. It also stated that MICR clearing should be set up in all branches of all the ones banks with more than a hundred branches.

In 1995, the Committee for offering law on electronic funds transfer and

---

[10]The Impact of Information Technology Adoption on the Customers of Bank of India, Bangalore Urban – An Evaluative Study *available at:* http://www.iosrjournals.org/iosr-jbm/papers/Vol17-issue3/Version-1/D017313944.pdf (Visited on October 15, 2017)

other digital payments (1995) once more emphasized EFT device.

Automated teller machine growth

the overall variety of automatic teller machines (ATMs) installed in India with the aid of diverse banks as of end June 2012 turned into 99,218.the new personal region banks in India have the maximum ATMs, followed via off-website ATMs belonging to SBI and its subsidiaries and then via nationalized banks and overseas banks, even as on-web site is highest for the nationalized banks of India.

Cheque truncation initiative

In 2008 the Reserve financial institution of India brought a gadget to allow cheque truncation in India, the cheque truncation gadget because it turned into acknowledged was first rolled out in the national Capital vicinity and then rolled out nationally.

Expansion of banking infrastructure

Virtual expansion of banking thru cell banking, net banking, and phone banking, biometric and cellular ATMs is taking area seeing that closing decade and has won momentum in last few years.

1.5 Various Forms of E-Banking:

Automated Teller Machines

A system that lets in customers of a banking organization to transact banking commercial enterprise with none assists of a cashier i.e. human clerk or human financial institution teller. ATM is likewise known as computerized banking gadget.

An automated teller system is an automatic telecommunications tool. With rapid boom in facts generation sector in from the beyond decade, every day new innovations are taking area in market. In financial area especially the banking quarter there are such a lot of new technologies are taking region in financial operations.

ATM is an essential invention for banking quarter. The improvements of current and information technology have made it possible for financial institution customers to engage and perform banking facility with computerized teller device and to obtain the cash immediately from the device or make deposit which include tests without help of person automatic teller gadget is a part of electronic banking and is new offerings that are being presented with the aid of at gift by most of banks in core banking region to its customers digital banking offers other services also other than computerized Teller system inclusive of direct enterprise deal buy/ sale thru point-Of-Sale (POS) and telephone banking and so forth one of the essential reasons for banks greater tendencies closer to automatic teller machine is each day growing fee of putting in and working financial institution department whether or not complete-fledged branch or extension counters and it has cause sharp boom in automated teller machine being installed via the banks, automated Teller Machines have found its fast reputation now not simplest due to low in banks transactions fees however also due to clients comfort and thereby it's miles emerge as want of the day in common guy's existence.[11]

There's usually two sides of a coin, the automated Teller Machines which enables the clients with the aid of presenting higher provider is has additionally darker aspect. some of clients have confronted cheating and frauds through computerized Teller Machines through withdrawals, withdrawal from their account now not transited through consumer himself and thereby customer have a while ugly revel in by using customers. Its miles undertaking now for the producers of automated teller system how to decrease the frauds for

---

[11] The Various Forms Of E Banking Information Technology Essay *available at:* https://www.ukessays.com/essays/information-technology/the-various-forms-of-e-banking-information-technology-essay.php (Visited on October 15, 2017)

maintaining automatic teller machine in functioning with its popularity being kept intact.

1.5.1 India's First ATM Card Fraud[12]

The Chennai City Police have busted an international gang involved in cyber crime, with the arrest of Deepak Prem Manwani (22), who was caught red-handed while breaking into an ATM in the city in June last, it is reliably learnt. The dimensions of the city cops' achievement can be gauged from the fact that they have netted a man who is on the wanted list of the formidable FBI of the United States. At the time of his detention, he had with him Rs 7.5 lakh knocked off from two ATMs in T Nagar and Abhiramapuram in the city. Prior to that, he had walked away

---

[12]"PINs and needles: Enter ATM hacking", *The Times of India,* Sep 15, 2003

with Rs 50,000 from an ATM in Mumbai.

While investigating Manwani's case, the police stumbled upon a cyber crime involving scores of persons across the globe. Manwani is an MBA drop-out from a Pune college and served as a marketing executive in a Chennai-based firm for some time. Interestingly, his audacious crime career started in an Internet cafe. While browsing the Net one day, he got attracted to a site which offered him assistance in breaking into the ATMs. His contacts, sitting somewhere in Europe, were ready to give him credit card numbers of a few American banks for $5 per card. The site also offered the magnetic codes of those cards, but charged $200 per code.

The operators of the site had devised a fascinating idea to get the personal identification number (PIN) of the card users. They floated a new site which resembled that of a reputed telecom companies. That company has millions of subscribers. The fake site offered the visitors to return $11.75 per head which, the site promoters said, had been collected in excess by mistake from them.

Believing that it was a genuine offer from the telecom company in question, several lakh subscribers logged on to the site to get back that little money, but in the process parted with their PINs. Armed with all requisite data to hack the bank ATMs, the gang started its systematic looting. Apparently, Manwani and many others entered into a deal with the gang behind the site and could purchase any amount of data, of course on certain terms, or simply enter into a deal on a booty-sharing basis. Meanwhile, Manwani also managed to generate 30 plastic cards that contained necessary data to enable him to break into ATMS.

He was so enterprising that he was able to sell away a few such cards to his contacts in Mumbai. The police are on the lookout for those persons too.

On receipt of large-scale complaints from the billed credit card users and banks in the United States, the FBI started an investigation into the affair and also alerted the CBI in New Delhi that the international gang had developed some links in India too. Manwani has since been enlarged on bail after interrogation by the CBI. But the city police believe that this is the beginning of the end of a major cyber crime.

Tele Banking

Assignment a bunch of banking associated offerings which include financial transactions from the ease of customers preferred region anywhere across the globe and any time of day and night has now been made thinkable via introducing online Tele banking offerings. By way of dialing the given Tele banking number via a landline or a mobile from everywhere, the consumer can get right of entry to his account and via following the user-pleasant menu; whole banking may be completed via Interactive Voice reaction (IVR) device. With sufficient numbers of looking traces made to be had, customer call will rarely fail. The device is bi-lingual and has following centers provided[13]:

1. Automatic balance voice out for the default account.

2. Balance inquiry and transaction inquiry.

3. Inquiry of all term deposit accounts.

4. Statement of account by Fax, e-mail or ordinary mail.

5. Cheque book request.

6. Stop payment which is on-line and instantaneous.

---

[13] S Arputharaj, "Advantages and Disadvantages of Mobile Banking In India " Special Issue *NCEBSED* 73 (2016)

7. Utility Bill Payments.

8. Renewal of term deposit which is automatic and instantaneous.

9. Voice out of last five transactions.

Smart Card

A smart card generally incorporates an embedded eight-bit microprocessor (a kind of laptop chip). The microprocessor is below a contact pad on one facet of the card think of the microprocessor as changing the standard magnetic stripe gift on a credit score card or debit card. The microprocessor at the smart card is there for security. The host computer and card reader simply "talk" to the microprocessor. The microprocessor enforces access to the facts on the card. The chips in these playing cards are capable of many varieties of transactions. For example, someone ought to make purchases from their credit score account, debit account or from a stored account price that is reloadable. The enhanced reminiscence and processing capability of the smart card is typically that of traditional magnetic-stripe cards and may accommodate numerous one of kind programs on a single card. It is able to additionally hold identification records; this means that no more shuffling through playing cards in the pockets to discover the proper one, the smart Card might be the handiest one wished. Clever cards also can be used with a clever card reader attachment to a personal computer to authenticate a consumer. Clever playing cards are very popular in Europe than inside the U.S. In Europe the medical health insurance and banking industries use smart cards notably. Every German citizen has a smart card for medical insurance. Even though smart playing cards had been round in their current shape for at the least a decade, they are just starting to take off inside the U.S. In India they're not famous now.[14]

---

[14]The Various Forms Of E Banking Information Technology Essay *available at:* https://www.ukessays.com/essays/information-technology/the-various-forms-of-e-banking-information-technology-essay.php (Visited on October 21, 2017)

Debit Card

Debit playing cards also are known as test playing cards. Debit cards seem like credit score cards or ATM (automated teller device) cards, but function like cash or a personal check. Debit playing cards are different from credit playing cards. While a credit score card is a way to "pay later," a debit card is a way to "pay now." when you operate a debit card, your cash is speedy deducted out of your checking or savings account. Debit cards are regularly occurring at many places, along with grocery stores, retail stores, gas stations, and restaurants. You can use your card everywhere traders display your card's brand call or brand. They offer an alternative to sporting a cheque e book or coins. In India debit card services are provided with the aid of nearly all the banks. Debit card service is one of the most fast growing offerings in India.

Internet Banking: E-Banking

E-banking is an abbreviation for digital banking. E-banking is generally implies for a carrier which allows clients to have account-precise information and additionally probable behavior transactions from a far off location the use of computer ready with network. A person can use this facility from any remote locations be it domestic or one's place of business. It lets in a consumer to behavior online bank transactions and the client need not to go to either his own bank or need of touring an automated teller machine. E-Banking is the automatic shipping replacing conventional advent 5 banking system and fulfills the customer's requirements via electronic centers i.e. e-community that is interactive channels for verbal exchange. E-banking is a structure of banking enabling monetary organization and its customers, be it individuals or agencies establishment to have get right of entry to its debts, freedom to transact commercial enterprise as properly to obtain statistics of the financial products and services using network either non-public or public. Net .customers may have got right of entry to e-banking offerings which uses shrewd electronic device. Such digital device may be a non-public computer, or a personal virtual assistant or an automatic teller gadget or digital kiosk, with touch tone Smartphone facilities. Electronic banking is also called on its feature as digital funds switch (EFT), thereby switch funds immediately from one account to every other account through using easy electronic centers.

[15]It enables you handle many banking transactions thru your non-public computer. as an instance, you can use your laptop to view your account balance, request transfers between bills, and pay bills electronically, internet banking system is a technique in which a personal pc is connected through a network provider without delay to a bunch laptop device of a bank such that customer support requests may be processed

15 Supra Note 11

mechanically without need for intervention by customer support representatives. The device is able to distinguishing between those customer service requests that are capable of computerized fulfillment and people requests which require coping with by using a customer service representative. The gadget is included with the host pc machine of the financial institution so that the far flung banking client can access other automated services of the financial institution. The approach of the intervention includes the steps of inputting a consumer banking request from among a menu of banking requests at a far flung personnel pc, transmitting the banking requests to a bunch laptop and receiving it, figuring out the type of purchaser banking request acquired, computerized logging of the service request, evaluating the received request to a stored table of request types, every of the request types having an characteristic to signify whether or not the request kind is capable of being fulfilled by means of a customer support representative or by means of an automated machine and depending upon the characteristic, directing the request both for coping with the aid of a customer support consultant or to a queue for processing by means of an automated device.

1.5 Internet Banking versus Traditional Banking

In spite of so many facilities that Internet banking offers us, we still seem to trust our traditional method of banking and is reluctant to use online banking. But here are few cases where Internet banking will turn out to be a better option in terms of saving the money.

'Stop payment' done through Internet banking will not cost any extra fees but when done through the branch, the bank may charge you Rs 50 per cheque plus the service tax through Internet banking, customers can check the transactions at any time of the day, and as many times as they want to. On the other hand, in a traditional method, one gets quarterly statements from the bank and if they request for a statement at the required time, it may turn out to be an expensive affair. The branch may charge Rs 25 per page, which includes only 30 transactions. Moreover, the bank branch would take eight days to deliver it at the doorstep. If the fund transfer has to be made outstation, where the bank does not have a branch, the bank would demand outstation charges. Whereas with the help of online banking, it will be absolutely free for you. As per the Internet and Mobile Association of India's report on online banking 2006,"

There are many advantages of online banking. It is convenient, it isn't bound by operational timings, there are no geographical barriers and the services can be offered at a miniscule cost."[16]

---

[16] Online Banking Vs. Traditional Banking *available at:* http://smallbusiness.chron.com/online-banking-vs-traditional-banking-5001.html (Visited on October 15, 2017)

CHAPTER - II
Nature, concept, scope of E-Banking system and Laws

2.1 Law of Banking

Banking law is based on a contractual analysis of the relationship between the bank and the customer—defined as any entity for which the bank agrees to conduct an account.[17]

The law implies rights and obligations into this relationship as follows:

• The bank account balance is the financial position between the bank and the customer: when the account is in credit, the bank owes the balance to the customer; when the account is overdrawn, the customer owes the balance to the bank.

• The bank agrees to pay the customer's cheques up to the amount standing to the credit of the customer's

---

[17] The Institute of Company Secretaries of India, *Study Material to Banking Law and Practice*, (ICSI, Delhi, 2016)

account, plus any agreed overdraft limit.

• The bank may not pay from the customer's account without a mandate from the customer, e.g. cheques drawn by the customer.

• The bank agrees to promptly collect the cheques deposited to the customer's account as the customer's agent, and to credit the proceeds to the customer's account.

• The bank has a right to combine the customer's accounts, since each account is just an aspect of the same credit relationship.

• The bank has a lien on cheques deposited to the customer's account, to the extent that the customer is indebted to the bank.

• The bank must not disclose details of transactions through the customer's account—unless the customer consents, there is a public duty to disclose, the bank's interests require it, or the law demands it.

- The bank must not close a customer's account without reasonable notice, since cheques are outstanding in the ordinary course of business for several days.

These implied contractual terms may be modified by express agreement between the customer and the bank. The statutes and regulations in force within a particular jurisdiction may also modify the above terms and/or create new rights, obligations or limitations relevant to the bank-customer relationship.

2.2 E-Banking in India

The trends taking location in statistics and verbal exchange technology are growing competition in financial institutions global. Consequently, the deployment of advanced technology is vital to acquire a competitive area. Recently, the banking enterprise was noticeably stricken by the technological revolution that transformed the manner banks supply their offerings, the usage of technologies including computerized teller machines, telephones, the net, credit cards, and electronic coins.

This venture covers the introduction and diffusion of retail banking and the development in electronic delivery channels and fee systems in its market that is termed as E-Banking.[18]

Digital banking is an umbrella term for the method via which a consumer may additionally carry out banking transactions electronically without touring any institution. The following phrases all talk to one shape or every other of digital banking: private computer (computer) banking, internet banking, virtual banking, online banking, domestic banking, far flung electronic banking, and get in touch with Banking. Pc banking and internet or on line banking is the maximum often used designations. It must be stated, however, that the phrases used to describe the diverse forms of digital banking are regularly used interchangeably.

[18] Supra Note 2

E-banking these days is the one of the quickest growing developments in Indian banking and is poised to take the banking sector a notch better. No extra falling in line in banks, no extra waiting lots of hours inside the financial institution, no greater days and weeks of ready. All can be accomplished with one card, on gadget. It's clean, it really works, and most importantly, humans adore it but nonetheless, some humans are having a tough time using this form of era, often people who are used to do matters the antique traditional way.

With using advertising, people are actually motivated to apply E-banking because again, it gets rid of the problem encountered whilst the usage of the old process of banking. The development of digital banking or usually known as e-banking, began with the usage of automatic teller machines (ATMs) and has included telephone banking, direct invoice fee ,electronic fund transfer, online banking and other digital transactions. for plenty human beings, they accept as true with that the e-banking will go to the path of cellular banking. also, some human beings believe that online banking may be the maximum popular technique in the future in order for users/customers to apply their bank's online offerings, they need to have a personal laptop and a web connection Additionally, their private computer systems might be their assistant who will help them in their transactions and offerings. Examples of those transactions are paying payments, obtaining data about bills and loans, and so forth. E-Banking (an abbreviation for electronic banking) is an umbrella time period for the system by way of which a patron might also carry out banking transactions electronically without journeying a brick-and-mortar institution. In simple terms, it does now not contain any bodily alternate of money, but it's all done electronically, from one account to every other, the use of the net. From a personal laptop, you may access bank account facts, and carry out many banking features, like transferring cash, creating a mortgage price.

Electronic banking, also called digital fund transfer (EFT), makes use of laptop and electronic technology as an alternative for tests and different paper transactions. In simple words, the structures that enable monetary organization customers, people or companies, to get admission to accounts, transact commercial enterprise, or gain facts on monetary services and products via a public or private network, including the internet i.e. pc, ATM, on line banking, and many others . It way any person with a personal laptop and a browser can get related to his bank -s internet site to carry out any of the digital banking features. In net banking device the financial institution has a centralized database that is internet-enabled. all the offerings that the financial institution has authorized on the net are displayed in menu. Any service may be selected and similarly interaction is dictated by using the nature of carrier.

The traditional branch version of bank is now giving place to an opportunity transport channels with ATM community. As soon as the branch workplaces of financial institution are interconnected via terrestrial or satellite TV for pc links, there could be no bodily identification for any branch. It would a without borders entity permitting each time, anywhere and anyways banking.

Definition of E-Banking

E-banking is described as the computerized delivery of new and traditional banking products and services at once to customers through electronic interactive communication channels. It includes the structures that allow monetary institution clients, people or businesses, to get entry to debts, transact business, or attain facts on financial products and services thru a public or nonpublic network, together with the internet. Customers access e-banking services the use of a sensible electronic device, together with a laptop, personal digital assistant, ATM, touch tone cell phone. E-banking is the term that describes all transactions that take place among corporations, agencies, and people and their banking organization.[19]

2.3 Adaptation of E-Banking in India[20]

The IT revolution had a notable impact within the Indian banking gadget. The usage of computer systems headed to creation of online banking in India. The use of the contemporary innovation and computerization of the banking area of India has improved many folds after the monetary liberalization of 1991 as the United States of America's banking sector has been exposed to the arena's marketplace. The Indian banks have been finding it difficult to compete with the international banks in terms of the customer service without the use of the facts technology and computers. The RBI in 1984 shaped Committee on Mechanization within the Banking enterprise (1984) whose chairman become Dr C Rangarajan , Deputy

---

[19] *ibid*

[20] Dr. Roshan Lal, Dr. Rajni Saluja (eds.) "E-Banking: The Indian Scenario " 1.4 *APJMM* 16 (2012)

Governor, Reserve bank of India. The fundamental guidelines of this committee had been introducing MICR (Magnetic Ink character reputation) generation in all the banks is the town in India. This supplied use of standardized cheque paperwork and encoders. In 1988, the RBI installation Committee on Computerization in Banks (1988) headed through Dr.C.R.Rangarajan which emphasized that settlement operation ought to be automatic within the clearinghouses of RBI in Bhubaneshwar , Guwahati, Jaipur, Patna and Thiruvananthapuram. It similarly said that there ought to be national Clearing of inter-town cheques at Kolkata , Mumbai, Delhi, Chennai and MICR must be made Operational. It also centered on computerization of branches and growing connectivity amongst branches thru computers. It additionally suggested modalities for enforcing online banking .The committee submitted its reports in 1989 and computerization commenced from 1993 with the agreement among IBA and bank personnel' affiliation. In 1994, Committee on technology troubles relating to bills system, Cheque Clearing and Securities agreement inside the Banking industry (1994 changed into set up with chairman Shri WS Saraf, government Director, Reserve financial institution of India. It emphasized on digital price range switch (EFT) machine, with the BANKNET communications community as its carrier. It also said that MICR clearing need to be set up in all branches of all banks with extra than 100 branches. Committee for offering legislation on electronic finances switch and different digital payments (1995) emphasized on EFT device.

Digital banking refers to doing banking by means of the use of technology like computers, internet and networking, MICR,EFT as a way to boom efficiency, brief service, productiveness and transparency within the transaction.

E-banking has sure capabilities which offer it facet over conventional banking:

Real Time Banking

Unlike traditional banking which suffers from time consuming procedures, E-Banking provides real time banking to the customers. You get all the relevant information about your account instantly. You can access all the details about your account sitting at home or at any distant location.

24/7 Banking

E-banking has eliminated the time constraint from banking. Now you could withdraw coins or get any banking facility every time.

Banking from everywhere: Don't fear if you are sitting in center East u .s .and want to test your account in New York. E-Banking in reality leaves no room for blaming the distances. Clever banking is prepared to serve you anywhere, anytime.

Safe and Secure Banking

Electronic- banking is more immune to security and safety related problems. Password Based Encryption (PBE), Secure Socket Layer (SSL), electronic signatures and electronic tokens gives a high level of security. Any malfunctioning or any inconsistency in your account can be traced easily. This makes E-Banking more reliable.

Easy Loans, Instant Loans

Use of smart cards, debit cards, credit cards has eased you from hatred, time consuming loaning procedures. Your banks provide you instant loans. No need to keep cash with you at all, a small chip card has replaced piles of cash. Certain web sites provide facility of online loaning. You can get instant loan there, just by filling a small form.

High Performance and Flexibility

E-Banking is a high performance system satisfying its customers for their every banking related queries

84

and desires. What makes it more interesting is its flexibility. Banking is using everyday advancements in technology, which makes it smart and banking system of today and tomorrow.

E-banking is an abbreviation for digital banking. E-banking is generally implies for a carrier which allows clients to have account-precise information and additionally probable behavior transactions from a far off location the use of computer ready with network. A person can use this facility from any remote locations be it domestic or one's place of business. It lets in a consumer to behavior online bank transactions and the client need not to go to either his own bank or need of touring an automated teller machine. E-Banking is the automatic shipping replacing conventional advent 5 banking system and fulfills the customer's requirements via electronic centers i.e. e-community that is interactive channels for verbal exchange. E-banking is a structures of banking enabling monetary organization and its customers, be it

85

individuals or agencies establishment to have get right of entry to its debts, freedom to transact commercial enterprise as properly to obtain statistics of the financial products and services using network either non-public or public net .customers may have get right of entry to e-banking offerings which uses shrewd electronic device. Such digital device may be a non-public computer, or a personal virtual assistant or an automatic teller gadget or digital kiosk, with touch tone Smartphone facilities. Electronic banking is also called on its feature as digital funds switch (EFT), thereby switch funds immediately from one account to every other account through using easy electronic centers.

It enables you handle many banking transactions thru your non-public computer. As an instance, you can use your laptop to view your account balance, request transfers between bills, and pay bills electronically. Internet banking system is a technique in which a personal pc is connected through a network provider without delay to a bunch laptop device of a bank such that customer support requests may be processed mechanically without need for intervention by customer support representatives. The device is able to distinguishing between those customer service requests that are capable of computerized fulfillment and people requests which require coping with by using a customer service representative. The gadget is included with the host pc machine of the financial institution so that the far flung banking client can access other automated services of the financial institution. The approach of the intervention includes the steps of inputting a consumer banking request from among a menu of banking requests at a far flung personnel pc, transmitting the banking requests to a bunch laptop and receiving it, figuring out the type of purchaser banking request acquired, computerized logging of the service request, evaluating the received request to a stored table of request types, every of the request types having an characteristic to signify whether or not the request kind is capable of being fulfilled by means of a customer support representative or by means of an automated machine and depending upon the characteristic, directing the request both for coping with the aid of a customer support consultant or to a queue for processing by means of an automated device.[21]

2.4 Services and facilities through E-Banking[22]

Online Applications

Consumers can begin their banking relationship with an online application. No need to waste time driving to a local branch to begin a banking relationship. Consumers can fill out and submit electronically all necessary information needed to open a checking, savings account or even a fixed deposit. When the application is

[21] *ibid*

[22] E-Banking in India: Services available in E-Banking and it's Practical Uses *available at:*
http://www.yourarticlelibrary.com/banking/e-banking-in-india-services-available-in-e-banking-and-its-practical-uses/23498 (Visited on October 22, 2017)

submitted, the bank will mail a signature card for its records and request one to mail or wire your initial funds. Some firms like American Express enable customers applying for an account to fund their new account electronically via a credit card or cheque from another banking institution.

Access to Accounts

Internet banking customers now have the ability to view their accounts online, including checking, savings, loans and credit cards. No need to wait for your monthly statements or wait in queue for the next available customer service representative. Account access enables customers to view most recent activity on accounts, including cleared checks, deposits, ATM transactions and balances as of previous day's activities. Customers no longer have to hold on to the cleared checks, since their bank will store them for them online.

24/7 Customer Support

Although it is easy to yield to the temptation of allowing the Internet to replace expensive branch personnel and overhead, many banks have found that a customer service staff ready at any hour is well worth the expense. This can be especially true as customer's transition to online banking and need help learning the features. Offering telephone and email a contact is a basic level of service. Offering live chat assistance is the exceptional level.

Access to the Old Transactions

Choices made in designing the Internet interface may include how much history will be available online. Some banks have chosen to show only 30-45 days, while others offer a history of six months or a year.[23]

Categorize Transactions and Production of Reports

Functionality is king as online banking customers using these

---

[23] *ibid*

features enjoy a Web interface that delivers the utility of a money management software application.

Export your Banking Data

Most banks offering the management interface also allow easy downloading of financial information into files that can be imported into Microsoft Money and Intuit's Quicken.

Interactive Guides & Tools to Help Selection of Proper Product

Although online, interactive guides through a bank's products, adds complexity to the programming it also serves the bank by assisting potential customers in choosing new products or services. Interactive Tools to design a savings plan, choose a mortgage, obtain online insurance quotes all tied to applications These tools help remove some of the mystery involved in so many account options and costs.

Status of Loans and Credit Card Account Information

Bank customers are familiar with reviewing their checking account information, but many banks are adding the ability to look at one's loan status and credit card information as well. Access to as many accounts held at the bank seems to be the goal.

View Digital Copies of Cheques

This, again, is removing a downside to online banking. It makes images of checks available as replacement for sending out cancelled cheques or sheets of printed cheque images.

Online Forms for Ordering Cheques, Stop Payment, etc.

Convenience is popular and if a customer visits his or her online account frequently it only makes sense to allow the ability to reorder cheques or perform certain other commands through the same interface.

Bill Payment Service

Customers can facilitate payment of electricity and telephone bills, mobile phone, credit card and insurance premium bills as each bank has tie-ups with various utility companies, service providers and insurance companies, across the country. To pay the bills, all one need to do is complete a simple one-time registration for each biller. Customers can also set up standing instructions online to pay their recurring bills, automatically. Generally, the bank does not charge customers for online bill payment.[24]

Fund Switch

Customers can transfer any amount from one account to another of the same or any other bank. Customers can send money anywhere in India. After login to the account, customers need to mention the payees' account number, his bank and the branch. The transfer will take place in a day or so, whereas in a traditional method, it takes about three working days. ICICI Bank says that online bill payment service and fund transfer facility have

---

[24] *ibid*

been their most popular online services.

Investing through Internet Banking

You can now open an FD online through funds transfer. Now investors with interlinked demat account and bank account can easily trade in the stock market and the amount will be automatically debited from their respective bank accounts and the shares will be credited in their demat account. Moreover, some banks even give you the facility to purchase mutual funds directly from the online banking system. Nowadays, most leading banks offer both online banking and demat account. However if you have your demat account with independent share brokers, then you need to sign a special form, this will link your two accounts.

Recharging your Prepaid Phone

Now customers can just top-up the prepaid mobile cards by logging into Internet banking. By just selecting the operator's name, entering the mobile number and the amount for recharge, the phone is again back in action within few minutes.

Shopping

With a range of all kind of products, customer can shop online and the payment is also made conveniently through the account. Customer can also buy railway and air tickets through Internet banking.

Railway Pass

This is something that would interest all the common people. Indian Railways has tied up with ICICI bank and they can now make railway passes for local trains online. The pass will be delivered to the customer's doorstep. But the facility is limited to Mumbai, Thane, Nashik,Surat and Pune.

Credit Card Customers

With Internet banking, customers can not only pay their credit card bills online but also get a loan on their cards. If the customer lose credit card, they can also report lost card online. The Reserve Bank of India constituted a working group on Internet Banking. The group divided the Internet banking products in India into three types based on the levels of access granted. They are:

Information Only System

General purpose information like interest rates, branch location, bank products and their features, loan and deposit calculations are provided in the bank's website. There exist facilities for downloading various types of application forms. The communication is normally done through email. There is no interaction between the customer and bank's application system. No identification of the customer is done. In this system, there is no possibility of any unauthorized person getting into production systems of the bank through internet.

Electronic Information Transfer System

The system provides customer-specific information in the form of account balances, transaction details, and statement of accounts. The information is still largely of the 'read only' format. Identification and authentication of the customer is through password. The information is fetched from the bank's application system either in batch mode or off-line. The application systems cannot directly access through the internet.

Fully Electronic Transactional System

This system allows bi-directional capabilities. Transactions can be submitted by the customer for online update. This system requires high degree of security and control. In this environment, web server and application systems are linked over secure infrastructure. It comprises technology covering computerization, networking and security, inter-bank payment gateway and legal infrastructure.

CHAPTER - III
Legal Aspects of E-banking Operations in India

3.1 The Indian Experience of E-Banking[25]

India is still in the early stages of E-banking growth and development. Competition and changes in technology and lifestyle in the last five years have changed the face of banking. The changes that have taken place impose on banks tough standards of competition and compliance. The issue here is' Where does India stand in the scheme of E-banking.' E-banking is likely to bring a host of opportunities as well as unprecedented risks to the fundamental nature of banking in India. The impact of E- Banking in India is not yet apparent. Many global research companies believe that E-

---

[25] Dr. Geeta Sharma, "Study of Internet Banking Scenario in India " Volume 5, Issue 5, *IJERMT* 43 (2016)

banking adoption in India in the near future would be slow compared to other major Asian countries. Indian E-banking is still nascent, although it is fast becoming a strategic necessity for most commercial banks, as competition increases from private banks and nonbanking financial institutions. Despite the global economic challenges facing the IT software and services sector, the outlook for the Indian industry remains optimistic. The Reserve Bank of India has also set up a "Working Group on E-banking to examine different aspects of E-banking. The group focused on three major areas of E-banking i.e.

(1) Technology and Security issues

(2) Legal issues and

(3) Regulatory and Supervisory issues.

RBI has accepted the guidelines of the group and they provide a good insight into the security requirements of E-banking. The importance of the impact of technology and information security cannot be doubted .Technological developments have been one of the key drivers of the global economy and represent an instrument that if exploited well can boost the efficiency and competitively of the banking sector. However, the rapid growth of the Internet has introduced a completely new level of security related problems. The problem here is that since the Internet is not a regulated technology and it is readily accessible to millions of people, there will always be people who want to use it to make illicit gains. The security issue can be addressed at three levels.

The first is the security of customer information as it is sent from the customer's PC to the Web server.

The second is the security of the environment in which the Internet banking server and customer information database reside.

Third, security measures must be in place to prevent unauthorized users from attempting to long into the online banking section of the website .From a legal perspective, security procedure adopted by banks for authenticating users needs to be recognized by law as a substitute for signature.

In India, the Information Technology Act ,2000, in [26] provides for a particular technology (viz., the asymmetric crypto system and hash function) as a means of authenticating electronic record. Any other method used by banks for authentication should be recognized as a source of legal risk. Regarding the regulatory and supervisory issues, only such banks which are licensed and supervised and have a physical presence in India will be permitted to offer E-banking products to residents of India. With institutions becoming more and more global and complex, the nature of risks in the international financial system has changed.

The Regulators themselves who will now be paying much more attention to

---

[26] Section 3(2) of IT Act, 2000.

the qualitative aspects of risk management have recognized this .Though the Indian Government has announced cyber laws, most corporate are not clear about them, and feel they are insufficient for the growth of E-commerce. Lack of consumer protection laws is another issue that needs to be tackled, if people have to feel more comfortable about transacting online .Taxation of E-commerce transaction has been one of the most debated issues that are yet to be resolved by India and most other countries.

The explosive growth of e-commerce has led many executives to question how their companies can properly administer taxes on Internet sales. Without sales tax, online sellers get a price advantage over brick and mortar companies. While-commerce has been causing loss of tax revenues to the Government, many politicians continue to insist that the Net must remain tax-free to ensure continued growth, and that collecting sales taxes on Net commerce could restrict its expansion. A permanent ban on custom duties on electronic transmissions, international tax rules that are neutral, simple and certain and simplification of state and local sales taxes. The Central Board of Direct Taxes, which submitted its report in September 2001, recommended that e-commerce transaction should be taxed just like traditional commerce.

Also RBI is about to become the first Government owned digital signature certifying Authority in India. The move is estimated to initiate the electronic transaction process in the banking sector and will have far reaching results in terms of cost and speed of transactions between government- owned banks. Thus efficiency, growth and the need to satisfy a growing tech-survey consumer base are three clear rationales for implementing E-banking in India. The four forces-customers, technology ,convergence and globalization have the most important effect on the Indian financial sector and these changes are forcing banks to redefine their business models and integrate technology into all aspect of operation.

3.2 Obligation of Banks and E-Banking

There are certain obligations which the banker is supposed to fulfill. They are Banks have to maintain secrecy of customers account. This obligation dates back to 1924 where in a case popularly known as Tournier case, in which it was held that banker should not disclose customer's financial position and the nature and the details of his account to anybody, since it may affect his reputation, creditworthiness and business. Now with the advent of new technology, this obligation has become a difficult task for there are hackers who can operate others account. Bankers are not in a position to trace them. They come to know only when the customer informs them of some irregularity in their transaction. Hence, to meet out this obligation, banks have to update their technology to the requirement. Banks are also under obligation (public duty), to produce documents to the court whenever called for. In earlier days this was easy as the documents were either in printed or in written form and readily available with the banks. Banks keep these information's in electronic form as it is easier and cheaper to store and retrieve and also ensures speedier communication/transmission. [27]

Information Technology Act, 2000 was drafted to facilitate users of electronic communication similar to other paper based or oral testimony means. Records can be kept in electronic form. Electronic form means information generated, sent, received or stored in media, magnetic, optical, computer memory, microfilm, etc. Now in the eyes of law written records means electronic records which can be produced before the court like it was produced previously. [28] But banks have to

---

[27] M.L.Tannan, Tannan's, Banking Law and Practice in India, (20th Ed.), (New Delhi: India Law House, 2003), p.157

[28] Section 13 of Banking Companies (Acquisition and Transfer of Undertaking) Act, 1970.

reproduce the documents and store them properly. If the software is attacked with virus it washes of all the documents. Hence, banks have to carefully handle the electronic documents or else they will be accountable to the law. Obligation to verify forgery of signatures . Banks have to verify the signature of the customer before paying their cheques. This obligation is on the paying banker. The law is very strict; and in case of forgery the banker is liable. This is limited to traditional banking. Introduction of new technology has helped banker in storage and retrieval of signature of customers. Each signature card is scanned using a scanner that takes images of the signature and converts it into digital form which are then stored in the hard disk. When a cheque (traditional) is received for payment, the signature can be retrieved by the user.[29] What when the funds are transferred electronically? In case of electronic fund transfer, digital signatures are

---

[29] Section 89 of the Negotiable Instruments Act, 1881.

used which are in the form of code? These signatures are in electronic form attached to electronic record.[30] The obligation of the banker to verify the signature is continuing here for digital signature. Hence, the banker should adopt technology which can identify the sender by recognizing message originator, authentication and non reputable that affixes a coded message to the document.[31] It is used to sign the record. Banker has to maintain records of the digital signature and also educate the customer in this regard. The other obligation on the banker is to provide proper service to the customer. Otherwise the bank is answerable. Not providing proper service attracts Consumer Law which amounts to deficiency in providing service.[32] It has been held in Vimal Chandra Grover v. Bank of India[33],that banking is a business transaction of a bank and

---

[30] R.N.Chaudhary, Banking Laws, (1st Ed.), (New Delhi: Central Law Publications, 2009). p.377.

[31] Tournier v. National Provincial & Union Bank of England, (1924), K.B., 461.

[32] Section 4 of Bankers Books Evidence Act, 1891.

[33] AIR 2000 SC 2181, 2000 (2) BLJR 1604

customers of a bank are consumers within the meaning of Section 2(1) (d) (ii) of the Act. This obligation extends to electronic banking also.

3.3 Guidelines by RBI for Banks Regarding E-Banking

1. All banks, who propose to offer transactional services on the Internet, should obtain prior approval from RBI.
2. All applications of banks should have proper record keeping facilities for legal purposes.
3. Banks should designate a network and database administrator with clearly defined roles as indicated in the Group's report.
4. Banks should introduce logical access controls to data, systems, application software, utilities, telecommunication lines, libraries, system software, etc. Logical access control techniques may include user-ids, passwords, and smart cards.
5. Banks should have proper infrastructure and schedules for backing up data. The backed-up data should be periodically tested.

6. All applications of banks should have proper record keeping facilities for legal purposes.

7. Considering the legal position prevalent, there is an obligation on the part of banks not only to establish the identity but also to make enquiries about integrity and reputation of the prospective customer. Therefore, even though request for opening account can be accepted over Internet, accounts should be opened only after proper introduction and physical verification of the identity of the customer.

8. Banks should acquire tools for monitoring systems and the networks against intrusions and attacks. These tools should be used regularly to avoid security breaches. The banks should review their security infrastructure and security policies regularly and optimize them in the light of their own experiences and changing technologies.

9. Banks should have a security policy duly approved by the Board of Directors.

10.Banks must make mandatory disclosures of risks, responsibilities and liabilities of the customers in doing business through Internet through a disclosure template. The banks should also provide their latest published financial results over the net.[34]

3.4 Legal Risks and Compliances

Compliance and prison problems arise out of the fast increase in utilization of e-banking and the differences among digital and paper-based approaches. E-banking is a brand new transport channel wherein the laws and regulations governing the digital delivery of certain financial institution products or services may be ambiguous or nevertheless evolving. Particular regulatory and prison demanding situations include:

Uncertainty over criminal jurisdictions and which state's or

---

[34]Internet Banking in India: Guidelines, *available at:* https://www.rbi.org.in/scripts/NotificationUser.aspx?Id=414&Mode=0 (Visited on October 25, 2017)

country's laws govern a selected e-banking transaction, delivery of credit and deposit-related disclosures/notices as required by law or regulation, Retention of required compliance documentation for online advertising, packages, statements, disclosures and notices and established order of legally binding electronic agreements. Legal guidelines and policies governing customer transactions require specific kinds of disclosures, notices, or record keeping requirements. Those requirements also follow to e-banking, and federal banking companies maintain to update consumer legal guidelines and regulations to mirror the impact of e-banking and online patron relationships. A number of the criminal necessities and regulatory guidance that frequently follow to e-banking products and services encompass: Solicitation, collection and reporting of presidency monitoring information on applications and loans, as required by way of same credit possibility Act and domestic mortgage Disclosure Act.

Advertising necessities, customer disclosures, or notices required by the actual property settlement techniques Act (RESPA), reality in Lending, truth in savings and truthful Housing guidelines. Right and conspicuous show of FDIC or NCUA coverage notices

India is a signatory of WTO. The basic principles of WTO are Liberalization, Globalization and Privatization. Therefore, trade and commerce in India has been liberalized. Incidentally, the financial sector has also undergone major changes. With the advent of e-banking, India is facing unprecedented competition from the World at large. If technology is not updated in financial sector, international trade would be a distant dream. The deregulation of the banking industry coupled with the emergence of new technologies has enabled new competitors to enter the financial services market quickly and efficiently. Various provisions of law, which are applicable to traditional banking activity, are also applicable to internet banking. This does not overcome the problems, and therefore there is a need for introduction of more stringent rules and laws specifically to meet the problems of e-banking. The legal framework for banking in India is provided by a set of enactments, viz. The Banking Regulation Act, 1949, the Reserve Bank of India Act, 1934 and Foreign Exchange Management Act, 1999 are few among many such legislations. It is mandatory on the part of all entities to obtain a license from Reserve Bank of India under Banking Regulations Act, 1949 to function as bank. Different types of activities which a bank may undertake and other prudential requirements are provided under this Act. Reserve Bank of India has regulated acceptance of deposit by Non Banking Institutions also. Under the Foreign Exchange Management Act, 1999, Non Residential Indians can lend, open a foreign currency account or borrow from a bank in India including from a Non-Resident bank, except under certain circumstances provided under the law.

Besides, banking activities are also influenced by various enactments governing trade and commerce, such

Conspicuous webpage disclosures indicating that positive kinds of funding, brokerage, and insurance products supplied have certain associated risks, and they're now not insured through federal deposit coverage. customer identification applications, in addition to record retention and client notification necessities, required with the aid of the bank Secrecy Act patron identity procedures to determine whether or not transactions are prohibited through the office of overseas Asset manipulate (OFAC) and, when important, whether customers seem on any list of acknowledged or suspected terrorists or terrorist employer provided with the aid of any authorities organization shipping of privateness and decide-out notices through hand, through mail, or with patron acknowledgement of electronic receipt and record retention requirements of the equal credit opportunity Act and truthful credit score Reporting Act .establishments that provide e-banking offerings, both informational and transactional, anticipate a better degree of compliance hazard due to the changing nature of the technology, the speed at which mistakes can be replicated, and the frequency of regulatory changes to cope with e-banking issues.

3.4.1 Strategic Risk

A monetary organization's board and management ought to understand the risks related to e-banking services and examine threat control costs against the return on funding previous to presenting e-banking services. Bad e-banking making plans and funding decisions can increase a monetary group's strategic danger. Early adopters of recent e-banking offerings can set up themselves as innovators who expect the needs in their customers, however may additionally achieve this by way of incurring higher prices and multiplied complexity in operations. past due adopters may be capable of keep away from the better fee and introduced complexity, but do so at the risk of no longer meeting patron call for additional products and services. In dealing with the strategic risk related to e-banking services, economic establishments must broaden defined e-banking goals and should be aware of the subsequent: Adequacy of management information systems to tune e-banking utilization and profitability.

expenses worried in monitoring e-banking activities or prices involved in overseeing e-banking companies and era provider companies transport and pricing of services adequate to generate sufficient call for Retention of digital loan agreements and other electronic contracts in a format on the way to be admissible and enforceable in litigation Availability of team of workers to offer technical aid for interchange related to more than one running structures, web browsers, and verbal exchange gadgets opposition from different e-banking vendors and adequacy of technical, operational, or advertising support for e-banking services and products.

3.4.2 Reputation Risk

An institution's decision to offer e-banking services, especially the more complex transactional services, significantly increases its level of reputation risk. Some of the ways in which e-banking can influence an institution's reputation include:

Loss of trust due to unauthorized activity on customer accounts, Disclosure or theft of confidential customer information to unauthorized parties (e.g., hackers),Failure to deliver on marketing claims Failure to provide reliable service due to the frequency or duration of service disruptions Customer complaints about the difficulty in using e-banking services and the inability of the institution's help desk to resolve problems, and Confusion between services provided by the financial institution and services provided by other businesses linked from the website.

3.5 Initiatives by Government for Developing E-Banking[35]

For growth and development and to promote e-banking in India the Indian government and RBI have been taken several initiatives. The Government of India enacted the IT Act, 2000 with effect from October 17, 2000 which provided legal recognition to electronic transactions and other means of electronic commerce.

The Reserve Bank monitors and reviews the legal requirements of e-banking on a continuous basis to ensure that challenges related to e-banking may not pose any threat to financial stability of the nation.Dr. K.C. Chakrabarty Committee including members from IIM, IDRBT, IIT and Reserve Bank prepared the IT Vision Document- 2011-17, which provides an indicative roadmap i.e. guidelines to enhance the usage of IT in the banking sector. The Reserve

---

[35] Vikas Chauhan, Dr .Vipin Choudhary(eds.), "Internet Banking: Challenges and Opportunities in Indian Context" 3 *JMST* 34 (2015)

Bank is striving to make the payment systems more secure and efficient. It has advised banks and other stakeholders to strengthen the security aspects in internet banking by adopting certain security measures in a timely manner. RBI believes that the growing popularity of these alternate channels of payments (such as: Internet Banking, Mobile Banking, ATM etc.) brings an additional responsibility on banks to ensure safe and secure transactions through these channels. .

National Payments Corporation of India (NPCI) was permitted by the RBI to enhance the number of mobile banking services and widen the IMPS (Immediate Payment Service) channels like ATMs, internet, mobile etc. Along with this, NPCI is also working to bring more mobile network operators which can provide mobile banking services through a common platform. On the recommendations of the Damodaran Committee, the guidelines were induced by RBI that provide internet banking as totally secured and protected, zero-liability against loss for any customer induced transaction & multi-lateral arrangements among banks to deal with internet banking frauds.

To deal with online banking frauds, customer can approach with their complaints to Banking Ombudsman. Under this Banking Ombudsman Scheme 2006, a customer can file their complaint against any deficiencies in banking service including internet banking, credit cards & ATM .

The Basel Committee on Banking Supervision's (2001) has defined risk management principles for electronic banking. They primarily focus on how to extend, adapt, and tailor the existing risk-management framework to the electronic banking setting.

CHAPTER – IV

Laws relating to E-banking

4.1 Overview

The road to electronic banking has not been smooth. Technology has played a pivotal role in all the sectors and banking was no exception to it. There are numerous advantages due to invention of e-banking. These advantages have attracted customers who want easy access to their accounts as well as safety. In India the safety is regulated by the Reserve Bank of India. RBI from time to time has been providing guidelines to all the banks incorporated in India to regulate their business in era of globalization. Apart from this, law has also extended its hands to safeguard the interest of the customer of the bank.[36]

---

[36] Law Relating to E-Banking in India – an outreach challenge *available at:* http://jsslawcollege.in/wp-content/uploads/2013/05/LAW-RELATING-TO-E-BANKING-IN-INDIA-%E2%80%93-AN-OUTREACH-CHALLENGE.pdf (Visited on October 25, 2017)

Electronic banking (e-banking) in India is seen as a viable and alternative mechanism to do traditional banking business. Even banking customers are happy to use the same for reasons of efficiency and time saving. However, there are many e-banking security related issues that are not paid attention to by Indian banks.

Law cannot possibly be expected to keep pace with changes in technology. The recent debacle of virtual voyeurism has brought out, amongst other things, the inadequacy and vulnerability of the laws governing use of internet. Fixing liability, recording and reproducing evidence, ascertaining jurisdiction are problems which show little sign of easing. Concerns over security and misuse pertaining to e-banking activity have been mounting as more banks in India foray into electronic banking. Though there was a message to banks that they should be formed for public good, since inception, banking has always been a commercial venture, the prime motive of banks being to enlarge profits. And lately adoption of new economic environment such as liberalization, privatization and globalization has caused concern in banking sector. Indian banks have also undergone a sweeping change where deregulation, technological innovations and globalization are significantly affecting the banking services. The emergence of internet banking has made many banks to rethink their Information Technology (IT) strategies in competitive markets. It is suggested that the banks that fail to respond to the emergence of internet banking in the market are likely to lose customers and that the cost of offering internet banking services is less than the cost of keeping branch banking. India has great prospect compared to other developing nations to leverage the potential of E-Banking and build a cash light economy. In addition to IT edge and relatively dense population, the Government of India (GOI) has clearly determined to achieve financial inclusion and is taking aggressive steps to see this happens. Rendering financial services to the un-served or poor through a market led approach is important for sustainability of financial inclusion. There are many reforms and enrollment drives which have been undertaken by the Reserve Bank of India (herein referred as RBI) and GOI in matter of financial inclusion over the last decade. The RBI and GOI policy initiatives and reforms have considerably helped the development of E-Banking system. The reforms include adoption of technology prototypes like smart cards, mobile based options, debit cards and credit cards. These facilities and advancement have given vent to more market driven environment, which is in fact, the future face of the Indian economy. Adoption of new technology has resulted in risks . The legal risk is one which arises from violation of, or nonconformance with laws, rules, regulations, prescribed practices, or when the legal rights and obligation of the transaction are not based on well established norms. Given the relatively new nature of internet banking, rights and obligations in certain cases are uncertain and applicability of laws and rules is also ambiguous. Other reason for legal risks is also uncertainty about the validity of agreements formed via electronic media and law relating to customers disclosure and privacy protection. A customer, who is inadequately informed about his rights and obligation, may not take proper precaution while using internet banking products or services, leading to disputed transactions, unwanted suits against the bank or other regulatory authority.

To cope with the risks on one hand and pressure of growing competition on the other has become inevitable to Indian banks. The banks have adopted several initiatives to curb the risk and also to play a safe in the competition world. The competition has been especially tough for the public sector banks (PSBs), as the newly established private sector and foreign banks have already sharpened their competitive edge. Some of the proactive PSB's have been striving hard to make their structures flexible enough to accommodate technological changes.

To regulate the banking in India there are many statutes, which forms the legal framework such as

1. Banking Regulation Act,1949,
2. The Reserve Bank of India Act,1934,
3. The Negotiable Instruments Act, 1881,
4. The Indian Contract Act, 1882,
5. Foreign Exchange Management Act, 1999,
6. Consumer Protection Act, 1986,
7. Prevention of Money Laundering Act, 2002,
8. Bankers Books Evidence Act, 1891,
9. Indian Evidence Act, 1872,
10. Indian Penal Code, 1860,
   The Payment and Settlement Systems Act, 2007 and most importantly

Information Technology Act,2000 to look into crimes committed due to E-Banking.

4.2 Information Technology Act, 2000

This is the pivotal legislation dealing with crimes committed due to technology in India. Technological innovation in general and IT applications in particular, have had a major effect in banking and finance. The technology and security standards are of prime important as the entire base of Internet banking rests on it. If the technology and security standards are inadequate, then Internet banking will not provide the desired results and will collapse ultimately. The adoption of firm's available new technology has been recognized as an important part of the overall process of technological change.

Information security is concerned with the protection of three characteristics of information, confidentiality, integrity and availability through the use of technical solutions and managerial actions. The IT Act 2000 was amended in 2008 enlarging definitions, introducing the concept of

128

electronic signature, creating new offences, and many more things.

IT Act, 2000 had only two sections dealing with computer related offences generally. The amended Act provides for a stronger data protection measures as well as strengthening the general framework against cyber crimes. There are certain issues which are inherent in the very nature of crimes committed by using IT which are specifically applicable to banker and customer. They are anonymity in cyberspace, the issue as to jurisdiction, the question of reliability and procuring of evidence and the issue of non-reporting of cyber crimes to authorities due to the bad publicity to the business.

The issues that are specific to banker and customer, apart from the above, are enlisted below-

1. **Intermediary-** From times immemorial banker and customer relationship consisted of multiple roles such as debtor and creditor, agent and principal, bailer and bailee,

trustee and beneficiary, which were called as general and special relationship between banker and customer. With the innovation in technology and adoption of it by the banker has created a new role to the banker as 'intermediary' and in certain respect as a 'data/information owner'.

The definition of 'intermediary' under IT Act, 2000, means 'any person who on behalf of another person receives stores or transmits that message or provides any service with respect to that message'. Though the banks are not directly referred to in the definition, the term is very wide to cover the banker, as the banker receives payments on behalf of the customers by receiving electronic messages. The same procedure applies for making payments on behalf of the customer which are normal activities of the banker. This renders them as intermediaries. Further, the definition also covers any person who provides any service with respect to such messages/records, in which case it is possible that banks may fall within the definition of the term 'intermediary'.

The definition was amended in 2008. The amended definition reads intermediaries as 'intermediary with respect to any particular electronic records, means any person who on behalf of another person receives, stores or transmits that record or provides any service with respect to that record and includes telecom service providers, network service providers, internet service providers, web hosting service providers, search engines, online payment sites, online-auction sites, online marketplaces and cyber cafes'.

The amendment does not really change the position of banks as intermediary but now even electronic records maintenance and transmission makes banks as intermediaries for E-Banking. The IT Act places some responsibilities on intermediaries such as secure the ETransactions, password and pay with due diligence.

In Sanjay Kumar Kedia v. Central Bureau and Anr, Supreme Court held that the service providers (intermediaries) are not liable for act done with due diligence. Whatever it is, uncertainty whether banker is an intermediary or not is not in the interest of the customer. Only thing is banker should act judiciously in case of E-Banking transaction.

2.   **Encryption**-The Central Government may, for securing the use of the electronic medium and for promotion of E-governance and E-commerce, prescribe the modes or methods for encryption. This is because any data which is transferred online is subject to the risk of being intercepted and misused.

Encrypting data before transferring it over the internet will go a long way in safeguarding against such interception. But such interception will not be of any use unless it is decrypted. If encryption of data is adopted by internet service providers, it will be helpful in protecting the customer's' privacy and also protection of all other data's. Internet Service Provider license restricts the level of encryption for individuals, groups or organizations. For banks RBI has stipulated a Secure Sockets Layer (SSL).

3. **Data Protection**- Data Protection refers to the set of privacy laws, policies and procedures that aim to minimize intrusion into one's privacy caused by the collection, storage and dissemination of personal data. Personal data generally refers to the information or data which relate to a person who can be identified from that information or data whether collected by any Government or any private organization or an agency.

IT Act imposes civil and criminal liability on a body corporate who is possessing, dealing or handling any sensitive personal data or information, and is negligent in implementing and maintaining reasonable security practices resulting in wrongful loss or wrongful gain to any person, then such body corporate may be held liable to pay damages to the person so affected.

It is important to note that there is no upper limit specified for the compensation that can be claimed by the affected party in such circumstances. It is in the discretion of the court to grant compensation to the victim.

The Act prescribes the punishment if any person who, in pursuance of the powers conferred under the IT Act, 2000, has secured access to any electronic record and information without the consent of the person concerned discloses such information to any other person, then he shall be punished with imprisonment up to two years or with fine up to one lakh or with both. Section 72A on the other hand provides the punishment for disclosure by any person, including an intermediary, in breach of lawful contract. The purview of Section 72A is wider than section 72[37] and extends to disclosure of personal information of a person (without consent) while providing services under a lawful contract and not merely disclosure of

---

[37] Information Technology Act, 2000.

information obtained by virtue of powers granted under IT Act, 2000.

As of now, the issue of data protection is generally governed by the contractual relationship between the parties, and the parties are free to enter into contracts to determine their relationship defining the terms personal data, personal sensitive data, data which may not be transferred out of or to India and mode of handling the same. Many a time the data is leaked or fraud is carried with the help of employee of the bank also. Internal threats can stem from three areas: the application development department, the infrastructure, and the data center. Despite the risk of internal threats, it is highly believed that threats from employees are largely unintentional. Threats from the employees results in misappropriation and embezzlement of funds.

4. **Computer related offences and Penalty/Punishment** -The IT Act, 2000 as amended, exposes the banks to both civil and criminal liability.

The civil liability could consist of exposure to pay damages by way of compensation up to five crores under the amended IT Act before the Adjudicating Officer and beyond five crores in a court of competent jurisdiction. There could also be exposure to criminal liability to the top management of the banks given the provisions of Chapter XI of the amended IT Act and the exposure to criminal liability could consist of imprisonment for a term which would extend from three years to life imprisonment as also fine. Phishing is one such offence which is covered.

5. **Bank's to be licensed as Certifying Authority**-Banks shall be allowed to apply for a license to issue digital signature certificate and function as certifying authority for facilitating Internet banking and that Reserve Bank of India shall issue the license under clause (o)[38].

The authentication of electronic records for the purposes of Internet banking should be in accordance with

---

[38] Section 6(1) of the Banking Regulations Act, 1949

the provisions of the Act. The electronic records duly maintained for the purposes of Internet banking would be recognized as legally valid and admissible.

The digital signature affixed in a proper manner would satisfy the requirement of signing of a document for the purposes of Internet banking. A digital signature meeting the specified requirements would be deemed to be a secured digital signature for carrying out Internet banking transactions. Digital signatures share some interesting features with legal signatures in the sense that they can be fairly readily and intimately related to an individual and they serve to authenticate digital content with a high degree of assurance.

Any kind of paper work, which is required to be filed in the government offices or its agencies, would be deemed to be duly filed if it is filed in the prescribed electronic form. Thus the paper formalities can be effectively substituted with electronic filings for Internet banking purposes. The records are maintained in electronic form. And then each bank can also publish rules, regulations, order, bye-laws, notification or any other matter pertaining to its business in electronic format.

If electronic record is sent by the originator or by his agent or by an information system programmed by or on behalf of the originator to operate automatically, then the electronic record shall be attributed to the originator. The requirement of acknowledgement of documents sent for the purposes of Internet banking is adequately safeguarded by the Act. The Internet banking may require to determine the time and place of dispatch and receipt of electronic records. The Internet banking would require the secured electronic records for its proper working.

Where any security procedure has been applied to an electronic record at a specific point of time, then such record shall be deemed to be a secure electronic record from such point of time to the time of verification. The

CG has the power to prescribe the security procedures to give effect to the provisions of the Act, having regard to the commercial circumstances prevailing at the time when the procedure was used. Thus, the CG can specify safety measures and security procedures for Internet banking under the provisions of the Act.

The Controller of Certifying Authorities can issue licenses to the Certification Authority under the IT Act, 2000. The Certifying Authority is assisted by the Registration Authority, which is created at the level of the organizations subscribing to the services of the Certifying Authority . The Reserve Bank would function as a Registration Authority for the proper functioning of Internet banking.

Thus, the IT Act, 2000 has laid down the basic legal framework conducive to the Internet banking in India. It must be noted that the object of the Act is to facilitate e-commerce and e-governance, which is essential for the functioning of the internet banking.

Table showing Offences and Punishment under IT Act, 2000 with regards to crimes against Electronic Banking

Section	Particulars	Punishment
Section 43	If a person without the permission of the owner or any one in charge of a computer system or network, secures access to such computer, downloads, copies or extracts data stored therein, introduces viruses or	He shall be liable to pay damages by way of compensation to the person so affected.

	contaminants into the system, damages and/or disrupts the computer system, denies access to a person authorized to access the computer, tampers with the computer system, destroys, deletes or alters information in a computer system,	
Section 66B	Receiving a stolen computer resource.	Up to 3 years imprisonment, fine up to

		Rs 1 lakh or both.
Section 66C	Identity theft.	Up to 3 years imprisonment, fine up to Rs 1 lakh.
Section 66D	Cheating by impersonation	Up to 3 years imprisonment, fine up to Rs 1 lakh
Section 66E	Violation of privacy, video voyeurism.	Up to 3 years imprisonment, fine up to Rs 2 lakhs

		or both.
Section 66F	Cyber Terrorism.	Life Imprisonment.
Section 67	Publishing or transmitting obscene material in electronic form.	Up to 10 years imprisonment with fine up to Rs 2 lakhs
Section 71	Misrepresentation and Suppression of material facts	Up to 2 years imprisonment with fine of Rs. 1 lakh or both.
Section 74	Publication for fraudulent	Up to 2 years

	purpose	impris onmen t with fine of Rs. 1 lakh or both
Section 85	Criminal liability of top bank management for various computer related offences	Minim um 3 years impris onmen t and maxi mum life impris onmen t

Apart from the above, the following important sections have been substituted and inserted by the IT Amendment Act, 2008:

Section 67C – Preservation and Retention of information by intermediaries - This is related to matter for storing information in

144

electronic form. Banks as intermediaries are required to store electronic information for some time as prescribed by RBI and report the same in its audit report.

Section 69 and 69A– Powers to issue directions for interception or monitoring or decryption of any information through any computer resource – If the Controller is satisfied that it is necessary or expedient so to do in the interest of the sovereignty or integrity of India, the security of the State, friendly relations with foreign States or public order or for preventing incitement to the commission of any cognizable offence, for reasons to be recorded in writing, by order, direct any agency of the Government to intercept any information transmitted through any computer resource.

Section 69B – Power to authorize to monitor and collect traffic data or information through any computer resource for cyber security. The cyber police or investigating authority has been authorized to collect data or information that is necessary to monitor the flow of data within or outside the country. Banks have to provide the same to the authority whenever called for.

Section 72A – Punishment for Disclosure of information in breach of lawful contract- The person disclosing shall be punished with imprisonment for a term which may extend to two years, or with fine up to one lakh rupees, or with both.

Section 79 – Exemption from liability of intermediary in certain cases- No person providing any service as a network service provider shall be liable under this information or data made available by him if he proves that the offence or contravention was committed without his knowledge or that he had exercised all due diligence to prevent the commission of such offence or contravention.

Section 84A – Modes or methods for encryption shall be prescribed by the CG. Section 84B –Punishment for abetment of offences- But no express provision made for the length of punishment for abetment to commit an offence under the law.

Section 84C –Punishment for attempt to commit offences - The section reads 'Whoever attempts to commit an offence punishable by this Act or causes such an offence to be committed, and in such an attempt does any act towards the commission of the offence, shall, where no express provision is made for the punishment of such attempt, be punished with imprisonment of any description provided for the offence, for a term which may extend to one-half of the longest term of imprisonment provided for that offence, or with such fine as is provided for the offence or with both. The length of punishment is not explicit in the provision and is left to the discretion of the court.

4.2.1 First Case Convicted under Information Technology Act 2000 of India.[39]

The case related to posting of obscene, defamatory and annoying message about a divorcee woman in the yahoo message group. E-Mails were also forwarded to the victim for information by the accused through a false e-mail account opened by him in the name of the victim. The posting of the message resulted in annoying phone calls to the lady in the belief that she was soliciting. Based on a complaint made by the victim in February 2004, the Police traced the accused to Mumbai and arrested him within the next few days. The accused was a known family friend of the victim and was reportedly interested in marrying her. She however married another person. This marriage later ended in divorce and the accused started contacting her

---

[39] The State of Tamil Nadu Vs Suhas Katti

148

once again. On her reluctance to marry him, the accused took up the harassment through the Internet. On 24-3-2004 Charge Sheet was filed u/s 67 of IT Act 2000, 469 and 509 IPC before The Hon'ble Addl. CMM Egmore by citing 18 witnesses and 34 documents and material objects. The same was taken on file in C.C.NO.4680/2004. On the prosecution side 12 witnesses were examined and entire documents were marked.

The Defense argued that the offending mails would have been given either by ex-husband of the complainant or the complainant herself to implicate the accused as accused alleged to have turned down the request of the complainant to marry her. Further the Defense counsel argued that some of the documentary evidence was not sustainable under Section 65B of the Indian Evidence Act. However, the court based on the expert witness of Na'vi and other evidence produced including the witness of the Cyber Cafe owners came to the conclusion that the crime was conclusively proved.

The court has also held that because of the meticulous investigation carried on by the IO, the origination of the obscene message was traced out and the real culprit has been brought before the court of law. In this case Sri S. Kothandaraman, Special Public Prosecutor appointed by the Government conducted the case. Honorable Sri.Arulraj, Additional Chief Metropolitan Magistrate, Egmore, delivered the judgment on 5-11-04 as follows: "The accused is found guilty of offences under section 469, 509 IPC and 67 of IT Act 2000 and the accused is convicted and is sentenced for the offence to undergo RI for 2 years under 469 IPC and to pay fine of Rs.500/-and for the offence u/s 509 IPC sentenced to undergo 1 year Simple imprisonment and to pay fine of Rs.500/- and for the offence u/s

67 of IT Act 2000 to undergo RI for 2 years and to pay fine of Rs.4000/- All sentences to run concurrently."

4.3 Reserve Bank of India Act, 1934[40]

In 1995, the Reserve Bank had set up the Committee for Proposing Legislation on Electronic Funds Transfer and other Electronic Payments. Based on the recommendation, the Reserve Bank of India Act, 1934 (hereinafter referred as RBI Act, 1934) was amended to include electronic banking operation.

A new clause [41], relating to the regulation of funds transfer through electronic means between banks, i.e. transactions like Real Time Gross Settlement (RTGS) and National Electronic Funds Transfer (NEFT) and other funds transfer was inserted, to facilitate such EFTs and ensure legal admissibility of documents and records. RBI encouraged electronic payment system has introduced

---

[40] Supra Note 34

[41] Section 58(2) of the RBI Act, 1934.

Electronic Clearing Service (ECS) and EFT system in 1995, the RTGS system in 2004, NEFT system in 2005 and Cheque Truncation System (CTS) in 2008.

ECS is an electronic mode of payment / receipt for transactions that are repetitive and periodic in nature. ECS is used by institutions for making bulk payment of amounts towards distribution of dividend, interest, salary, pension, or for bulk collection of amounts towards telephone / electricity / water dues, cess / tax collections, loan installment repayments, periodic investments in mutual funds, insurance premium and other receipts. Essentially, ECS facilitates bulk transfer of money from one bank account too many bank accounts or vice versa. ECS and EFT was introduced in the year 1995, RTGS was introduced in 2004 and NEFT was introduced in 2005 by amending RBI Act. System of truncation of cheques was also recognized by the RBI. Truncation is the process of stopping the flow of the physical cheque issued by a drawer to the drawee branch. The physical instrument will be truncated at some point en-route to the drawee branch and an electronic image of the cheque would be sent to the drawee branch along with the relevant information 192 like the MICR fields, date of presentation, presenting banks etc.

Thus with the implementation of cheque truncation, the need to move the physical instruments across branches would not be required, except in exceptional circumstances. This would effectively reduce the time required for payment of cheques and the associated cost of transit and delay in processing, thus speeding up the process of collection or realization of the cheques. CTS were introduced in 2008. Working group was constituted headed by Shri. G. Gopalakrishnan to study frauds due to electronic banking which gave its report. In the Report the committee has highlighted the danger of compliance or checklist type of mindset and called for dynamic and proactive assessment of various threats and their mitigation. One of the important aspects is the focus on "information security awareness", as it is acknowledged that people often represent the weakest link in the security chain.

In addition, the Report has called for enhancing the use of technology for identifying anomalous e-banking transactions, effective analysis of audit trails and logs, enhancing audit processes through the use of computer assisted audit tools, identifying vulnerabilities in systems and networks and using application systems for carrying out critical business processes involving financial/regulatory/legal and customer related implications rather than through manual methods or through spreadsheets. Meanwhile RBI has issued guidelines on Security Issues and Risk mitigation measures related to Card Present (CP) transactions. The highlights of this circular is measure has been taken to secure Card Not Present (CNP) transactions, making it mandatory for banks to put in place additional authentication/validation for all on-line recurring transactions based on information not available on the credit/debit /prepaid cards.

Accordingly, banks and other stakeholders are directed to initiate immediate action for accomplishing the following tasks within the time indicated. Implementation of improved fraud risk management practices and securing the technology infrastructure were the task assigned to the commercial banks in India. The target time given for the completing of the task was September, 2012.

With the Banking Laws Amendment Act, 2012, RBI is empowered to call for any information and cause inspection of business of any 'associate enterprise' of a bank. This has provided legal framework for setting up a Bank Holding Companies and paves the way for issue of new bank licenses. RBI has been issuing guidelines to the commercial banks on IT, electronic banking and technological risk management and cyber frauds.

4.4 Banking Regulation Act, 1949[42]

The Act originally came into force on 16th March, 1949 and it was known as Banking Companies Act, 1949. It was amended was renamed as Banking (Acquisition and Transfer of Undertaking) Act, 1969 and the original Act was extended to the cooperative banks from 1966 and is simply called as B.R.Act, 1949. The objectives of the Act are, to safeguard the interest of depositors, to develop banking institutions on sound lines and to attain the monetary and credit system to the larger interests and priorities of the nation. Amendment has been brought to the original legislation as regards acquiring of shares. An approval may be granted by the RBI if it is satisfied that the shares are acquired in the interest of public, or the in the interest of banking policy or to prevent the affairs of any banking company being conducted in manner detrimental to public interest or

---

[42] Banking Regulation Act, 1949, *available at:* http://fiuindia.gov.in/files/released_acts/banking_regu lation_act.html (Visited on October 25, 2017)

companies interest, or in the interest of the emerging trends in banking and international practices, or in the interest of banking and financial system in India. The applicant is the proper person to acquire shares or voting rights and no other person has such right. The voting right given under the law has immense power to the shareholders to control the banking business of the company. The RBI has exclusive power to issue, accept or reject application for license to carry on banking business. The RBI shall establish a Fund to be called the "Depositor Education and Awareness Fund".

The salient features of the Banking Laws (Amendment) Act, 2012 are-

1. Regulatory power to supersede board of banks Under the Banking Regulation Act, 1949 (hereinafter referred as B R Act, 1949) the RBI could remove a director or any other officer of the bank. RBI is empowered to supersede the board of directors of a bank for up 12 months if it feels that the board is not working in the interest of shareholders and depositors'. In

case the bank is not working in the interest of the shareholders or depositors, RBI shall carry on the business of the bank by appointing an administrator during the period. RBI now being armed with powers to supersede the Board, it can now effectively influence and regulate management of banks. To limit arbitrary exercise of power by the RBI, the Act provides for consultation with the Indian Government.

2. Inspect associate enterprises The Act empowers the RBI to call for any information and cause inspection of business of any 'associate enterprise' of a bank. This should provide legal framework for setting up of Bank Holding companies and pave the way for issue of new bank licenses. Associate enterprises could be a holding company or subsidiary company of the bank, a joint venture, an enterprise which controls the composition of the Board of Directors of the bank, an enterprise which influences the bank in taking financial decision or an enterprise which obtains economic benefits from the activities

of the bank. RBI may not be able to call for information from 'associate enterprises' incorporated outside India of foreign banks. However, the Indian branches and Indian associate enterprises of a foreign bank will fall under the RBI purview of 'associate enterprise' and they may call for information. An associate enterprise (outside India) of a foreign bank which has a Wholly-Owned Subsidiary (WOS) in India is covered under the Act.

3. Increase in voting rights in a public sector bank (PSB), no shareholder (except the Central Government) shall exercise voting rights in excess of one percent of the total voting rights of all the shareholders. Further, the preference shareholder (except the Central Government) also has an embargo on the voting rights up to one percent of total voting rights of all the shareholders holding preference share capital only. The Act raises the shareholders' voting rights in a public sector bank from one percent to 10 percent. No shareholder, in a private sector bank, can exercise voting rights

in excess of ten percent of the total voting rights of all the shareholders.

4. Conversion of a branch of a bank into Wholly Owned Subsidiary Conversion of a branch of any bank into a Wholly Owned Subsidiary (WOS) or transfer of shareholding of a bank to its holding company is now exempt from stamp duty. These amendments would be beneficial for various stakeholders in the banking sector. While the banking regulator gets enhanced powers that will result in effective compliance of regulations, banks will be able to attract more investments to raise funds for business expansion and to meet capital norms. Accounts and audit, is also very strict under the law. It is the auditor who should examine whether there is an effective system of obtaining confirmations/acknowledgement of debts periodically. For this purpose, the auditors should also review the branch audit reports. The auditor is expected to report on the following aspects of the recovery period, existence of a recovery policy, regular updating, monitoring and adherence,

compliance with the RBI guidelines and system of monitoring of recovery from credit card dues in respect of credit cards issued. The auditor is expected to give his observations on major frauds discovered during the year under the audit. The auditor is also expected to comment on the efficacy of the system and follow up on vigilance reports. According to R.B.Burman Committee recommendation the bank and financial institutions should conduct Information System Audit conforming to information system audit policy, which has been incorporated in the present system.

4.5 Negotiable Instruments Act, 1881

Under the Negotiable Instruments Act, 1881, cheque includes electronic image of truncated cheque and a cheque in the electronic form. The definition of a cheque in electronic form contemplates digital signature with or without biometric signature and asymmetric crypto system.

Cheque truncation, loosely defined, is the process in which the physical movement of cheque within bank, between banks and clearing house is curtailed or eliminated, being replaced in whole or in part, by electronic records of their content, with or without images, for further processing and transmission. The truncation of cheque in clearing has been given effect to and appropriate safeguards in this regard have been put forth in the guidelines issued from time to time. [43] Cheque Truncation speeds up the process of collection of cheques resulting in better service to customers reduces the scope for clearing-related frauds or loss of instruments in transit, lowers the cost of collection of cheques, and removes reconciliation-related and logistics-related problems, thus benefitting the system as a whole. The truncated cheque is an electronic image of the cheque. When it is presented for payment, the drawee

---

[43] Electronic Cheque (E-Cheque) and Truncated Cheque in India, *available at:* https://www.corporate-cases.com/2016/03/e-cheque-truncated-cheque.html (Visited on October 15, 2017)

bank is entitled to demand any further information regarding the truncated cheque from the bank holding the truncated cheque in case of any reasonable suspicion about the genuineness of the apparent tenor of instrument and if the suspicion is that of any fraud, forgery, tampering or destruction of the instrument, it is entitle to further demand the presentment of the truncated cheque itself for verification, provided that the truncated cheque so demanded by the drawee bank shall be retained by it, if payment is made accordingly.

This provision protects the paying banker who pays in good faith and without negligence. Truncation of cheques can be done by the clearing house or the bank which collects the truncated version of the cheque. As per Section 81[44], the banker who receives the payment is also supposed to retain the copy of the cheque even after payment has been done.

Section 89 of the NI Act says that any distinction between the original cheque and the truncated image should

---

[44] NI Act, 1881.

be construed as material alteration. A material alteration is one which varies the rights, liabilities, or legal position of the parties ascertained by the deed in its original state or otherwise varies the legal effect of the instrument as originally expressed, or reduces to certainty some provision which was originally ascertained and as such void, or may otherwise prejudice the party bound by the deed as originally executed. In such cases it is obligatory on the part of the clearing house or the bank to ensure the correctness of the truncated image while transmitting the image.

The Supreme Court of India has opined that there should be early disposal of cases relating to dishonor of cheques, enhancing punishment for offenders, introducing electronic image of a truncated cheque and a cheque in the electronic form as well as exempting an official nominee director from prosecution under the NI Act, 1881.

A certificate issued on the foot of the printout of the electronic image of a truncated cheque by the banker who paid the instrument, shall be prima facie proof of such payment. Where the cheque is an electronic image of a truncated cheque, any difference in apparent tenure of such electronic image and the truncated cheque shall be a material alteration and it shall be the duty of the bank or the clearing house, as the case may be, to ensure the exactness of the apparent tenure of electronic image of the truncated cheque while truncating and transmitting the image. Any bank or a clearing house which receives a transmitted electronic image of a truncated cheque, shall verify from the party who transmitted the image to it, that the image so transmitted to it and received by it, is exactly the same.[45]

NI Act makes an obligation on the banks to make payment in due course. Section 131 of the Act [46] has an explanation which states, 'it shall be the duty of the banker who receives payment based on an electronic image of a truncated cheque held with him, to

---

[45] Supra Note 44

[46] Negotiable Instruments (Amendment and Miscellaneous Provisions) Act, 2002

verify the prima facie genuineness of the cheque to be truncated and any fraud, forgery or tampering apparent on the face of the instrument that can be verified with due diligence and ordinary care'. In case of dishonor of cheque, the period for giving notice of dishonor has been extended to 30 days instead of 15 days.

Also any dispute in this matter shall be resolved within 2 years (instead of 1 Year) from the date of institution of the suit. Truncating cheques entails additional operational risks. Banks have to take adequate measures to ensure that all necessary safeguards are provided. It must be in consonance with the legal requirements and banking practice.

While making payment especially of high value instruments under the system extra care has to be taken, otherwise the banker will become liable under section 131 of the NI Act. But a clearing house cannot be held liable for fraud or forgery, as they cannot open the truncated cheques. In all cases the banker should act judiciously and within the purview of the law.

4.6 Other Relevant Acts

4.6.1 Bankers Books Evidence Act, 1891

Amendment is carried even to the Bankers Books Evidence Act, after the advent of E-Banking in India. Section 2 of the Act defines which books are 'banker's books'. This includes ledgers, day-books, cash-books, account-books and all other records used in the ordinary business of the bank, whether these records are kept in written form or stored in a microfilm, magnetic tape or in any other form of mechanical or electronic data retrieval mechanism, either onsite or at any offsite location including a backup or disaster recovery site of both. And a printout of any entry in the books of a bank stored in a microfilm, magnetic tape or in any other form of mechanical or electronic data retrieval mechanism obtained by a mechanical or other process which in itself ensures the accuracy of such printout as a copy is admissible as evidence. Certified copy means books in written form and has an attestation as 'true copy' and print out or data stored in a floppy, disc, tape or any other electronic magnetic storage system. The printout shall have certificate of bank manager and computer in-charge person. All these amendments have made the law applicable to cases relating to E-Banking when evidence is produced before the court of law or an arbitrator.[47]

4.6.2 Prevention of Money Laundering Act, 2002

Money laundering is the practice of engaging in financial transactions in order to conceal the identity, source, and/or destination of money, and is a main operation of the underground economy.

Money laundering is defined as the conversion or transfer of property, knowing that such property is derived

---

[47] Legal Relation of E-Banking in India *available at:* http://shodhganga.inflibnet.ac.in/bitstream/10603/148 886/12/12_chapter%205.pdf (Visited on October 15, 2017)

from serious crime, for the purpose of concealing or disguising the illicit origin of the property or of assisting any person who is involved in committing such an offence or offences to evade the legal consequences of his action, and the concealment or disguise of the true nature, source, location, disposition, movement, rights with respect to, or ownership of property, knowing that such property is derived from serious crime.[48]

In other words, the source of illegally obtained funds is obscured through a succession of transfers and deals in order that those same funds can eventually be made to appear as legitimate income. Every financial institution is charged with the responsibility of developing policies and procedures to combat money laundering, which includes the duty to be aware of trends and adaptations in the methods by which money laundering is carried out. The most

---

What is Money launderings?, *available at:* http://files.acams.org/pdfs/English_Study_Guide/Chapter_2.pdf (Visited on October 15, 2017)

difficult aspect of this responsibility is a financial organization's ability to anticipate new criminal behavior and to proactively implement protocols before the criminal behavior occurs.

Bankers play the most prominent role and without their connivance the operation on money laundering cannot be curtailed. Development of new high tech coupled with wire transfer of funds has further aggravated the difficulties to detect the movement of slush funds. As internet banking transactions are conducted remotely, banks may find it difficult to apply money laundering rules for some forms of electronic payments. Thus, banks expose themselves to the money laundering risk.

This may result in legal sanctions for noncompliance with 'know your customer' (KYC) rules. Every banking company, financial institution and intermediary, as the case may be, is required to maintain a record of transactions as prescribed by the rules and furnish information to the director within time prescribed under the law. The principal officer of the financial institution should furnish the information in writing or by fax or e-mail to the director. The records to be maintained by such entities are set forth in rule 3 of PMLR. Such records include record of cash transactions of value more than ten lakhs or its equivalent in foreign currency.

Integrally connected cash transaction which takes place within one month, of any forged or counterfeit note, or there is any suspicious transactions should also be reported every month before 15th day of the succeeding month. Such records are to be maintained by the financial institutions for ten years from the date of the transaction. The financial institution is also required to maintain the records and identity of their clients. The financial institution is required to formulate and implement a client identification programme and for this they may have their own additional requirements to determine the identity of the clients. A copy of the said identification programme is required to be forwarded to the director.

The above provision needs to be appreciated, though they are procedural in nature, it leads to maintenance of records and reporting of transactions which helps in tracking frauds, forgeries and money laundering and the persons involved in such transactions. The law is a penal law. It imposes penalty for every failure. This penalty may in addition to penalties imposed by other laws.

The officer incharge of and responsible to the conduct of the business shall be liable to be prosecuted and punished under this Act. It is therefore clear that such entities should have a robust system of keeping track of the transactions of the nature referred in the Act and the Rule and report the same within the prescribed period to the authority concerned. The fear to the financial institution is not just penalty, but reputation risk of the entity.

4.6.3 Indian Contract Act, 1872

The Indian Contract Act, is two century old law, but complete in all aspects relating to contracts including

E-contracts. For a valid contract there are certain requirements to be fulfilled which are, that there should be lawful consideration, the consent should be free, the persons entering into contract must be competent persons (they should not be minor, unsound mind or prohibited under law to enter into contract) and the contract should be made to achieve a lawful object.

The Act also deals with the different modes of discharge of contract and also special contracts. Apart from the above requirement, there should be proposal and an unconditional acceptance of the proposal. What one can infer from the above is that the contract enforceable under the law is a process, which has a vital significance in any transaction whether manufacturing or trading or service. The contract has to be valid contract to be enforceable.

E-contract is any kind of contract formed in the course of e-commerce by the interaction of two or more individuals using electronic means, such as email, the interaction of an individual with an electronic agent, such as a computer program, or the interaction of at least two electronic agents that are programmed to recognize the existence of a contract.

In E-Contracts the offer is not made directly to the customer. The consumer 'browses' the available goods and services displayed on the merchant's website and then choose what he would like to purchase. The offer is not made by website displaying the items for sale at a particular price. This is actually an invitation to offer and hence is revocable at any time up to the time of acceptance. The offer is accepted through e-mails or by just clicking 'I Agree'. [49]

The significance of the contract assumes importance in cyber world where anonymity and speed of transaction are key elements. Contracts entered through online process are called as electronic contracts.

---

[49]A study of Formation and challenges of electronic contract in cyberspace, *available at:* http://www.legalservicesindia.com/article/article/a-study-of-formation-and-challenges-of-electronic-contract-in-cyberspace-1943-1.html (Visited on October 27, 2017)

Electronic contracts helps people to avail the transactions and agreements electronically without meeting each other personally. In an electronic contract normally two parties are involved, the originator and the addressee. The originator is one who sends stores or transmits electronic messages. The message is transmitted to the 'addressee' is one whom the originator intends to receive the electronic record but does not include intermediary. Intermediary is a person who transmits, stores or receives message on behalf of another or provides any service in respect thereof. If we apply the above theory then in the terms of contract, the result is originator is the promissory; addressee is promise and intermediary is the service of carrier.

Electronic message/data can be transmitted without human intervention. As soon as the message is transmitted to the intermediary and is out of control of the originator, it is regarded as delivered. According to the IT Act [50], if the originator has

---

[50] Section 12 of the IT Act, 2000.

stipulated for acceptance (I agree) and if that for formalities is completed by the addressee, it becomes a binding/valid contract.

The legal requirement of signing the electronic document is also fulfilled by attesting digital signature through a private key assigned to the party by the certifying authority. This part concludes two aspects of contract that is proposal and acceptance. The third part is that the consent must be free that is it must not be taken by coercion, undue influence, fraud, misrepresentation, or by mistake.

Among them fraud is both civil wrong as well as criminal wrong. And in commercial transaction, fraud affects the most. In case of banker and customer relationship is a contractual relationship and hence after the advent of E-Banking fraud has played a pivotal role. Though Indian Contract has defined fraud, but the wrong is civil in nature. The person who has suffered injury or damage can claim only compensation.

Fraud committed on banks or by banks is criminal in nature because it involves a deceptive act perpetrated on a victim which is done for personal or financial gain. Hence, the definition of fraud as stated in contract law can be used only to know the meaning and claiming compensation.

E Banking is ultimately an E-Contract and all the provisions of Indian Contract Act applies to it muttas mundadis.

4.6.4 Indian Penal Code, 1860

Crime is both a social and economic phenomenon. It is as old as human society. In developing economies, cybercrime has increased at rapid strides, due to the rapid diffusion of the Internet and the digitization of economic activities. The improvement of online banking system and its increased use by consumers worldwide has made this service a privileged target for cyber criminals.

Sweeping amendments were made to certain provisions of Indian Penal Code (herein referred as IPC). Section 172 relating to documents to be produced before a Court of Justice includes electronic records, Section

192 or makes false entry in books of records, and section 463, the amendment is inserting false electronic record with the intent to cause damage or injury.[51]

The significant amendment was to section 464 of the Act which is as follows-'A person is said to make a false document or false electronic record, if,

First, who dishonestly or fraudulently makes, signs, seals or executes a document or part of a document, or makes or transmits any electronic record or part any electronic record, or affixes any digital signature on any electronic record, or makes any mark denoting the execution of a document or the authenticity of the digital signature, with the intention of causing it to be believed that such document or part of a document was made, signed, sealed or executed by or by the authority of a person by whom or by whose authority he knows that it was not made, signed, sealed or executed,

[51] AMENDMENTS TO THE INDIAN PENAL CODE, *available at:* http://www.cyberlawclinic.org/ipc.htm (Visited on October 30, 2017)

or at a time at which he knows that it was not made, signed, sealed or executed; or affixed with, or,

Secondly.- Who, without lawful authority, dishonestly or fraudulently, by cancellation or otherwise, alters a document or an electronic record in any material part thereof, after it has been made or executed or affixed with digital signature either by himself or by any other person, whether such person be living or dead at the time of such alteration; or

Thirdly.- Who dishonestly or fraudulently causes any person to sign, seal, execute or alter a document or an electronic record or to affix his digital signature on any electronic record knowing that such person by reason of unsoundness of mind or intoxication cannot, or that by reason of deception practiced upon him, he does not know the contents of the document or electronic record or the nature of the alteration. Then section 469, for the words "intending that the document forged" the words "intending that the document or electronic record forged" was substituted. Section 474, for the portion beginning with the words "Whoever has in his possession any document" and ending with the words "if the document is one of the description mentioned in section 466 of this Code", the following words were substituted, "Whoever has in this possession any document or electronic record, knowing the same to be forged and intending that the same shall fraudulently or dishonestly be used as a genuine, shall, if the document or electronic record is one of the description mentioned in section 466 of this Code.".IPC is a legislation which is probably the most widely used law in criminal jurisprudence, serving as the main criminal code of India.

Offences or crimes have been elaborately dealt under this legislation listing punishment for each offence. IT Act 2000 has amended the sections dealing with records and documents in the IPC by inserting the word 'electronic' thereby treating the electronic records and documents on par with physical records and documents.

The sections dealing with false entry in a record or false document are (ex. 192, 204, 378, 383, 463, 464, 468, 469, 470, 471, 474, 476, 499 etc) have since been amended as electronic record and electronic document thereby bringing within the ambit of IPC, all crimes to an electronic record and electronic documents just like physical acts of forgery or falsification of physical records.

Internet frauds in India are recent phenomena but over the years, it has emerged like an organized crime. Hackers may be anywhere in the world and employ any technique to commit the fraud. Even mobile transactions are hit by the frauds. There are three crucial elements which are considered responsible for the commission of frauds in banks: a. Involvement of bank's employee or in connivance with outsiders; b. Failure of the bank staff to follow the instructions and guidelines; and c. External elements or collusion between various parties or by a hacker.

Though there are various kinds of frauds, but purely from reporting standpoint, RBI has classified frauds on the basis of the provisions of the IPCa. Misappropriation (Section 403 IPC) and criminal breach of trust (Section 405 IPC); b. Fraudulent encashment through forged instruments, manipulation of books of account or through fictitious accounts and conversion of property (Sections 477A, 378 and 120 A); c. Unauthorized credit facilities extended for reward or for illegal gratification; d. Negligence and cash shortages; e. Cheating (Section 415 IPC) and forgery (Section 463 IPC); f. Forgery of electronic records (Section 465 IPC);g. Bogus websites, cyber frauds, phishing (Section 420 of IPC) h. Irregularities in foreign exchange transactions; and i. Any other type of fraud not coming under the specific heads as above. Though no specific section defines fraud, all the above provisions are related with the offence. The courts in India have dealt with E-Banking frauds combining sections of IPC and IT Act. Ex. Syed Asifuddin and Ors. v. The State Of Andhra Pradesh and others, where case was registered under Sections 409, 420 and 120B of IPC, 1860 and Section 65 of the IT, 2000, the court stated 'whoever knowingly or intentionally conceals, destroys or alters or intentionally or knowingly causes another to conceal, destroy, or alter any computer source code used for a computer, computer programme, computer system or computer network, when the computer source code is required to be kept or maintained by law for the time being in force, shall be punishable with imprisonment up to three years, or with fine which may extend up to two lakhs rupees or both.

Further, while giving explanation to section 65 of the IT Act it stated the word "dishonestly" shall have the meaning assigned to it in section 24 of the IPC and the word "fraudulently" shall have the meaning assigned to it in section 25 of the IPC. To mitigate this confusion, a definition of fraud was, however, suggested in the context of electronic banking in the Report of RBI Working Group on Information

Security, Electronic Banking, Technology Risk Management and Cyber Frauds, which reads as 'a deliberate act of omission or commission by any person, carried out in the course of a banking transaction or in the books of accounts maintained manually or under computer system in banks, resulting into wrongful gain to any person for a temporary period or otherwise, with or without any monetary loss to the bank'.

4.6.5 Indian Evidence Act, 1872

The enactment and adoption of the Indian Evidence Act was a path-breaking judicial measure introduced in India, which changed the entire system of concepts pertaining to admissibility of evidences in the Indian courts of law. The nature of evidence in the real world and virtual world is different. This disparity is conspicuous in all the stages of evidence detection, gathering, storage and exhibition before the court.

Contrary to the real world crimes, where tangible evidences in the form of fingerprints, weapon of crimes, blood stain marks, can be traced, in the virtual world such traces becomes very difficult to find. The process of preservation of cyber crime evidences lies within the understanding of an efficient and knowledgeable computer forensics expert because any carelessness in the process can lead to diminutive value of the evidence. Once the required evidence is identified than the investigator must ensure that the same is collected by adhering to the legal requirements.

The legal requirement are, evidence is collected only after the requisite warrant for is issued, if the information appears to be outside the scope of the warrant then additional warrant be issued, completion of the investigation, and other formalities. The evidence collected becomes valid in the court of law only if the evidence is collected by legal means.

The Indian Evidence Act was amended according to the requirements of the IT Act. The Indian Evidence Act gave recognition to all electronic records and documents. In the definition part of the Act, the amendment was made to the word documents which are as follows 'where the word all documents includes electronic records'. Words like 'digital signature', 'electronic form', 'secure electronic record', 'information' as used in the IT Act, were all inserted to make them part of the evidentiary mechanism in the legislation. The under section 17^{52}, for the words 'oral or documentary' the words 'oral or documentary or contained in electronic form was substituted. Then section 35 of the Act was amended for the word 'record', in both the places where it occurs, the words 'record or an electronic record' was substituted.

Section 39 of the original Act deals with evidence to be given when statement forms part of a conversation, document, book or series of letters or papers.- 'When any statement of which evidence is given forms part of a longer statement, or of a conversation or part of an isolated document, or is contained in a document which forms part of a book, or of a connected series of letters or

---

[52] IT Act, 2000.

papers, evidence shall be given of so much and no more of the statement, conversation, document, book or series of letters or papers as the Court considers necessary in that particular case to the full understanding of the nature and effect of the statement, and of the circumstances under which it was made'. The substituted wordings of the section, what evidence to be given when statement forms part of a conversation, document, electronic record, book or series of letters or papers- 'When any statement of which evidence is given forms part of a longer statement, or of a conversation or part of an isolated document, or is contained in a document which forms part of a book, or is contained in part of electronic record or of a connected series of letters or papers, evidence shall be given of so much and no more of the statement, conversation, document, electronic record, book or series of letters or papers as the Court considers necessary in that particular case to the full understanding of the nature and effect of the statement, and of the circumstances under which it was made'.

Section 47 was amended and **section 47A** which emphasis on the opinion as to relevancy of digital signature reads thus- 'when the court has to form an opinion as to the digital signature of any person, the opinion of the certifying authority which has issued the Digital Signature Certificate is a relevant fact'. Section 59 was also amended where the word 'contents of documents', were substituted with words 'contents of documents or electronic records'.

Section 65 was amended and two subsection section 65A and 65B were inserted. 65A deals with special provisions as to evidence relating to electronic record and 65B deals with admissibility of electronic records. The other amendments were relating to proof as to digital signature, proof as to verification of digital signature, presumption as to electronic records and digital signatures, presumption as to digital signature certificate, and production of documents or electronic records which another person, having possession, court refuses to produce before courts.

Amendments brought to Indian Evidence Act were questioned in P. Padmanabh v. Syndicate Bank Limited, where court held admissibility of electronic records, any information contained in an electronic record which is printed on a paper, stored, recorded or copied in optical or magnetic media produced by a computer (hereinafter referred as the computer output) shall be deemed to be also a document, if the conditions mentioned in this section are satisfied in relation to the information and computer in question and shall be admissible in any proceedings, without further proof or production of the original, as evidence of any contents of the original or of any fact stated therein of which direct evidence would be admissible.

Admissibility of electronic records as evidence as enshrined in **section 65B** of the Indian Evidence Act is wide enough to cover all types of electronic records as evidence which states as under- 'Any information contained in an electronic record which is printed on a paper, stored, recorded or copied in optical or magnetic media produced by a computer shall be treated like a document, without further proof or production of the original, if the conditions like these are satisfied:

(a) The computer output containing the information was produced by the computer during the period over which the computer was used regularly.... by lawful persons..

(b) The information ...derived was regularly fed into the computer in the ordinary course of the said activities;

(c) Throughout the material part of the said period, the computer was operating properly was out of operation during that part of the period, was not such as to affect the electronic record or the accuracy of its contents; and

(d) the information contained in the electronic record reproduces or is derived from such information fed into the computer in the ordinary course of the said activities' To put it in simple terms, evidences (information) taken from computers or electronic storage devices and produced as print-outs or in electronic media are valid if they are taken from system handled properly with no scope for manipulation of data. And thus ensuring integrity of data produced directly with or without human intervention accompanied by a certificate signed by a responsible person declaring as to the correctness of the records taken from a system a computer with all the precautions as laid down in the section.

4.6.6 Consumer Protection Act, 1986

Consumer protection in India got a boost with the enactment of Consumer Protection Act, 1986. It provided a power in the hands of Indian consumers to get appropriate, timely and effective grievances redressal against companies and individuals who had provided defective good or deficient services.

It has been most effective weapon in the hands of consumers for claiming compensation through speedy redressal. Speedy justice which is fundamental right of the citizens of

India has been guaranteed is ensured in this Act.

It is a board which is constituted and many of the formalities which are required to be followed in the normal courts need not followed. The justice is ensured by a bench headed by a chairman and two social workers who sit and listen to the matter. Both documentary and oral evidence are taken. Material objects are also examined and justice is ensured. Customer of a bank is also a consumer as he fits into the definition of consumer under the law.

Consumer is a person who buys or hires and goods or services for a consideration, i.e. free services are not covered under the Act. It excludes a person who buys or hires for commercial purpose/activity and not for self-consumption.

The National Consumer Forum has held that once it is found that there is hiring of service for consideration and that loss has been caused to the complainant on account of negligence and deficiency in rendering the service, the aggrieved consumer is entitled to seek remedy under Consumer Protection Act and the aggrieved consumer is also entitled to seek redressal from appropriate forum.

Technological failure and providing confidential details have been treated as deficiency of service in banks provided the customer has not acted negligently. The bank should give instruction to the customer before providing them with E-Banking facility. Internet banking has now started motivating customers to park their funds with the online banks, which has a substantially impact on the deposit base of the brick and

Mortar banks and the same should be encouraged with precautions.[53]

---

[53] Sharma Vijaykumar Ramchandra , "A Study of Consumer Protection Act Related to Banking Sector " 4 *APJMMR* 78 (2012)

CHAPTER - V

Problems faced by E-banking system in India

The challenges related to e-banking prevail in Indian context are discussed below[54]:

A. Security Risk: The problem related to the security has become one of the major concerns for banks. A large group of customers refuses to opt for e-banking facilities due to uncertainty and security concerns.
According to the IAMAI Report (2006), 43% of internet users are not using internet banking in India because of security concerns. So it's a big challenge for marketers and makes consumers satisfied regarding their security concerns, which may further increase the online banking use.

---

[54] Supra Note 35

B. Privacy risk: The risk of disclosing private information & fear of identity theft is one of the major factors that inhibit the consumers while opting for internet banking services. Most of the consumers believe that using online banking services make them vulnerable to identity theft. According to the study consumers' worry about their privacy and feel that bank may invade their privacy by utilizing their information for marketing and other secondary purposes without consent of consumers.

C. The Trust Factor: Trust is the biggest hurdle to online banking for most of the customers. Conventional banking is preferred by the customers because of lack of trust on the online security. They have a perception that online transaction is risky due to which frauds can take place. While using e-banking facilities lot of questions arises in the mind of customers such as: Did transaction go through? Did I push the transfer button once or twice? Trust is among the significant factors which influence the customers' willingness to engage in a transaction with web merchants.

D. Customer Awareness: Awareness among consumers about the e-banking facilities and procedures is still at lower side in Indian scenario. Banks are not able to disseminate proper information about the use, benefits and facility of internet banking. Less awareness of new technologies and their benefits is among one of the most ranked barrier in the development of e-banking.

E. Less Internet Penetration in Indian Context: The internet banking channel has evolved over the years. In 2011, 60 percent of the times basic transactions in banks were conducted in North America through online channels, whereas internet banking usage in India increased from 1 percent in 2006 to 7 percent in 2011. So the knowledge and availability of internet is still a one of the biggest challenges that prevails in Indian context.

According to the report of IAMAI 2006 around 22% of internet users do not have knowledge about transferring online. So the penetration of internet and knowledge related to internet are major hurdles.

Financial institutions, their card associations, and vendors are working to develop an Internet payment infrastructure to help make electronic commerce secure. Many in the banking industry expect significant growth in the use of the Internet for the purchase of goods and services and electronic data interchange. The banking industry also recognizes that the Internet must be secure to achieve a high level of confidence with both consumers and businesses.

Sound management of banking products and services, especially those provided over the Internet, is fundamental to maintaining a high level of public confidence not only in the individual bank and its brand name but also in the banking system as a whole. Key components that will help maintain a high level of public confidence in an open network environment include: Security Authentication Trust Non-repudiation Privacy Availability

197

Security is an issue in Internet banking systems. The office of the comptroller of currency (OCC) expects national banks to provide a level of logical and physical security commensurate with the sensitivity of the information and the individual bank's risk tolerance. Firewalls are frequently used on Internet banking systems as a security measure to protect internal systems and should be considered for any system connected to an outside network. Firewalls are a combination of hardware and software placed between two networks through which all traffic must 66 pass, regardless of the direction of flow. They provide a gateway to guard against unauthorized individuals gaining access to the bank's network. Authentication is another issue in an Internet banking system.[55]

Transactions on the Internet or any other telecommunication network must be secure to achieve a high level of public confidence. In cyberspace, as in the physical world, customers, banks, and merchants need assurances that

---

[55] *ibid*

they will receive the service as ordered or the merchandise as requested, and that they know the identity of the person they are dealing with.

Trust is another issue in Internet banking systems. As noted in the previously, public and private key cryptographic systems can be used to secure information and authenticate parties in transactions in cyberspace. A trusted third party is a necessary part of the process. That third party is the certificate authority. A certificate authority is a trusted third party that verifies identities in cyberspace.

Some people think of the certificate authority functioning like an online notary. The basic concept is that a bank, or other third party, uses its good name to validate parties in transactions. This is similar to the historic role banks have played with letters of credit, where neither the buyer nor seller knew each other but both parties were known to the bank. Thus the bank uses its good name to facilitate the transaction, for a fee.

Non-repudiation is the undeniable proof of participation by both the sender and receiver in a transaction. It is the reason for which the public key encryption was developed, i.e., to authenticate electronic messages and prevent denial or repudiation by the sender or receiver. Although technology has provided an answer to non-repudiation, cyber laws are not uniform in the treatment of electronic authentication and digital signatures. The application of cyber laws to these activities is a new and emerging area of the law. Privacy is a consumer issue of increasing importance. National banks that recognize and respond to privacy issues in a proactive way make this a positive attribute for the bank and a benefit for its customers. Public concerns over the proper versus improper accumulation and use of personal information are likely to increase with the continued growth of electronic commerce and the Internet. Providers who are sensitive to these concerns have an advantage over those who do not.

Availability is another component in maintaining a high level of public confidence in a network environment.

All of the previous components are of little value if the network is not available and convenient to customers. Users of a network expect access to systems 24 hours per day, seven days a week. Among the considerations associated with system availability are capacity, performance monitoring, redundancies, and business resumption.

National banks and their vendors who provide Internet banking products and services need to make certain they have the capacity in terms of hardware and software to consistently deliver a high level of service. In addition, performance monitoring techniques will provide management with information such as the volume of traffic, the duration of transactions, and the amount of time customers must wait for service. Monitoring capacity, downtime, and performance on a regular basis will help management assure a high level of availability for their Internet banking system.[56]

---

[56] *ibid*

5.1 Types of Fraud

5.1.1 Electronic Fraud

This refers to email scams from fraudsters to obtain banking and personal information and here is how it works: The person receives an email appearing to be from NBK Company or another legitimate company in or out of a country. The email may claim a number of different things such as: There is a problem with your account Ask you to enter a contest to win a prize Ask you to subscribe to a service that will provide you with prizes and etc. You are then asked to provide your personal and financial information by completing an online form. The form requests a variety of information such as: Your credit card numbers your account number your passport or Civil ID numbers and so forth once you provide this information the fraudsters will have the necessary information on you to conduct a fraud.

Numerous definitions of e-fraud have been advanced in the e-crimes literature. Graham (2001) defines e-fraud as "a fraudulent behavior connected with computerization by which someone intends to gain dishonest advantage". In this definition e-fraud equates to, and supersedes, the term computer fraud. Some definitions specify e-fraud in relation to electronic commerce or the Internet such as Smith (2001) in which e-fraud is seen as "any dishonest activity that involves the Internet as the target or means of obtaining some financial reward". The US Department of Justice also defines e-fraud in relation to the Internet. "A fraud scheme that uses one or more components of the Internet - such as chat rooms, e-mail, message boards, or web sites - to present fraudulent solicitations to prospective victims, to conduct fraudulent transactions, or to transmit the proceeds of fraud to financial institutions or to other connected with the scheme". Alternatively, some studies define such crimes as 'Internet fraud',[57]

---

[57] Fraud, *available at:*
https://legaldictionary.net/fraud/ (Visited on November 1, 2017)

5.1.2 Identity Fraud

Identity fraud is where a dishonest person will gather personal details in order to conduct a fraud which will financially hurt the user. These fraudsters can obtain user personal information in a number of ways, via telephone scams or on the internet.

The following can be used to assume customer identity: Date of birth Address Personal ID number or other identification numbers Mobile phone number banking information.

5.1.3 Spyware and Adware

Spyware is a type of software that secretly collects user personal and information while on the Internet. Adware is a type of spyware used to track visitors' habits and interests on the Internet. Adware can monitor the types of sites user visit, the articles read or the type's banners user click on and so forth. Many times this information is sold to a third party for the purpose of marketing.

5.1.4 Wire Fraud

Wire transfer networks such as the international, interbank fund transfer system are tempting as targets as a transfer, once made, is difficult or impossible to reverse. As these networks are used by banks to settle accounts with each other, rapid or overnight wire transfer of large amounts of money are commonplace; while banks have put checks and balances in place, there is the risk that insiders may attempt to use fraudulent or forged documents which claim to request a bank depositor's money be wired to another bank, often an offshore account in some distant foreign country.

5.1.5 Impersonation or Identity Theft

Theft of identity has become an increasing problem; the scam operates by obtaining information about a victim, then using the information to apply for identity cards, accounts and credit in that person's name. Often little more than name, parents' name, date and place of birth are sufficient to obtain a birth certificate; each document obtained then is used as identification in order to obtain more identity documents. Government-issued standard identification numbers such as PAN numbers are also valuable to the identity thief. Unfortunately for the banks, identity thieves have been known to take out loans and disappear with the cash, quite content to see the wrong persons blamed when the debts go bad.

Dishonest bank personnel have been known to disclose depositors' personal information for use in theft of identity frauds. The perpetrators then use the information to obtain identity cards and credit cards using the victim's name and personal information.

5.1.6 Credit Card Fraud

Credit card and debit card fraud is a crime where credit or debit cards are reproduced by criminals. This type of crime is known as 'skimming'. Credit or debit card fraud can also occur when user card is lost or stolen and used by fraudster to purchase goods or remove cash from ATMs or other locations.

Credit card fraud is a multi-billion-currency a year loss for banks and the government. With the progression of computers and e-commerce, hackers are able to exploit more information more easily without ever having to leave their homes. Now, entire departments of organizations in the criminal justice system are being dedicated to preventing and finding cyber-crimes.[58]

There are many ways that scammers can actually get user information. This can be as simple as mass sending an e-mail impersonating a bank and linking to a look-alike website luring you to enter your financial information there, or they can be as complicated as stealing information off the real bank website through complicated computer viruses. Financial institution look-alike websites can be found all over the internet, and can be very convincing. This method generally isn't very involved, as it is quite easy to design or find a website that remotely looks like bank institutions. This method has also been around the longest and has

[58] *ibid*

motivated financial websites to secure their websites more. The look-alike websites are coded to look and act likes the normal

.website, with one difference: The information submitted to the site goes to the hacker's databases rather than the banks.

Another method of obtaining financial information is ATM skimming. Popular recently, this method involves putting a mechanism on the ATM's card slot that reads that magnetic strip. If placed correctly, these machines can be very effective, because the user still is able to go through with their transaction on the ATM. The device has a small magnetic reader called an MSR, and a small memory card that records all cards inserted. Magnetic strips have two important strings of information on them, called Track 1 and Track 2. Although only one is needed for a bank transaction, both tracks are usually paired and exploited together. The more informative Track 1 contains account number, expiration date, card verification value (CVV2) code, and name of account holder.

This, of course, is all the information needed to steal money from the account holder. The data dumped from the memory cards, are called "dumps". Knowing store owners or other knowledgeable people, these dumps can be exploited.

In most cases, dumps are sold without PIN numbers, and only depending on the bank, only $500 can be stolen from the account. However, with a PIN number, the account could be completely emptied at the disposal of the hacker. Of course, greater payouts mean greater effort and risk involved. Retrieving PIN numbers is more involved and requires more advanced technology to retrieve. Dumps are the most complicated form of stolen financial information to cash out, as they require access to a bank wire that only retailers would have. This gets into money laundering and other ways to put on the facade that the money is being earned legitimately.

There is another method that involves using a money transfer service from legitimate money Transfer Company to transfer the money from the stolen account to a separate account. The obstacle hackers have to overcome is the fact that legitimate company operators check the identity of the bank account to the person executing the transaction. This can be overcome by knowing operators or possibly working with them. Operators that are involved with illegal sending of money are known as "drops", and share the profit with the hacker.

Finally, a more efficient and brute-force method is to steal online retailers' customer databases. Obviously, this is a gold mine of information for a hacker. In some cases, little effort is required to hack into insecure databases from smaller retailers and can result in massive payouts for the hacker with little effort. The data collected from this method usually can sell on the black market for a higher price, as the data is almost guaranteed to be accurate, and depending on the vendor, quality data can be sold for a varying price on the black market. In most cases, the hackers that exploit this financial information do not use it directly for financial gain. Instead, they sell the information. Hackers sell three basic things: "dumps" (track 1 and track 2 off the magnetic strips), "CVVs" (all information needed to buy something online), and "full" (a cvv plus social security number, mother's maiden name, date of birth, and PIN number). "CVVs" are usually the cheapest, ranging from $1.50 to $5 a piece, depending on the age of the information and the type of card (VISA, Mastercard, American Express, and Discover). "Fullz" usually sell for $8-$15 dollars, and finally "dumps" can sell for up to $100 depending on the seller.

Like anything, discounts are given for buying in greater quantities. One may be wondering how these exchanges are made. It has been described that the illegal credit card market is like the illegal drug market. The system works in a hierarchical way, prices vary, and there are scammers. Obviously, hackers can use the streets to sell ill-gotten information, through a chat-system called Internet Relay Chat, IRC. IRC is an extremely simple protocol of chat that has been around since the time the internet was invented, and by nature is extremely hard to monitor and track. The only time during which third parties such as the police can monitor chats through IRC, are when the actual exchange is occurring. After the exchange, there is absolutely no record of the chat.

There are IRC servers entirely dedicated to illegal credit card distribution, though contain no evidence to prosecute with. Also, every user usually is behind what is called a proxy. A proxy is a server that the user connects to and then uses to connect to the illegal server to avoid being traced. Properly run proxies are extremely hard to trace to the origin, and offer an extra layer of protection. Once connected to the server, users join what are called channels and find literally advertisements from vendors. Buyers find sellers, send them a message, and the exchange is executed. Other forms of communication are personal instant messengers such as Yahoo Messenger and regular e-mail.

Of course, hackers simply can't pay for the illegal data with conventional methods of internet payment. Hackers commonly use services such as EGOLD, Liberty Reserve, and other forms of electronic metal. Emetal accounts are bank accounts that are 100% backed by gold, silver, platinum, and other precious metals, and they are 100% untraceable and anonymous. Payments are made from one e-metal account to another, and nothing can be traced. Other forms of payment can include services such as Western Union and MoneyGram, and are used for larger purchases usually.

5.1.7 Booster Cheques

A booster cheque is a fraudulent or bad cheque used to make a payment to a credit card account in order to "bust out" or raise the amount of available credit on otherwise-legitimate credit cards. The amount of the cheque is credited to the card account by the bank as soon as the payment is made, even though the cheque has not yet cleared. Before the bad cheque is discovered, the perpetrator goes on a spending spree or obtains cash advances until the newly-"raised" available limit on the card is reached. The original cheque then bounces, but by then it is already too late.

5.1.8 Duplication or Skimming of Card Information

This takes a number of forms, ranging from a dishonest merchant copying clients' credit card numbers for later misuse (or a thief using carbon copies from old mechanical card imprint machines to steal the info) to the use of tampered credit or debit card readers to copy the magnetic stripe from a payment card while a hidden camera captures the numbers on the face of the card. Some thieves have clandestinely added equipment to publicly accessible automatic teller machines; a fraudulent card stripe reader would capture the contents of the magnetic stripe while a hidden camera would sneak a peek at the user's PIN. The fraudulent equipment would then be removed and the data used to produce duplicate cards that could then be used to make ATM withdrawals from the victims' accounts.

5.1.9 Money Laundering

The term "money laundering" dates back to the days of Al Capone Money laundering has since been used to describe any scheme by which the true origin of funds is hidden or concealed. The operations work in various forms. One variant involved buying securities (stocks and bonds) for cash; the securities were then placed for safe deposit in one bank and a claim on those assets used as collateral for a loan at another bank. The borrower would then default on the loan. The securities, however, would still be worth their full amount. The transaction served only to disguise the original source of the funds. The Finance ministers of G-20, including India has decided to take counter measures against tax havens particularly non-cooperative ones, to prevent money laundering and terror financing through cyber crimes from 2010.

5.2 Internet Banking Frauds

Internet Banking Fraud is a fraud or theft committed using online technology to illegally remove money from a bank account and/or transfer money to an account in a different bank. Internet Banking Fraud is a form of identity theft and is usually made possible through techniques such as phishing.

Now internet banking is widely used to check account details, make purchases, pay bills, transfer funds, print statements etc. Generally, the user identity is the customer identity number and password is provided to secure transactions. But due to some ignorance or silly mistakes you can easily fall into the trap of cyber criminals.

Here are some simple tips to prevent you from falling into the trap of cyber criminals. Remember, a simple ignorance or oversight can make a huge dent in your hard- earned savings.[59]

---

[59] Internet Banking Frauds ,*available at:* http://www.worldjute.com/ebank1.html (Visited on November 1, 2017)

Securing your account : Avoid online banking on unsecured wifi systems and operate only from PCs at home. Never reveal password to anyone. Do not even write it on a piece of paper on diary. Just memories it. It should be alphanumeric and change it frequently.

Never reply to queries from bank online about account or personal details. The personal information should not be kept in a public computer or in emails.

Phishing: A person's personal details are obtained by fraudsters posing as bankers, who float a site similar to that of the person's bank. They are asked to provide all personal information about themselves and their account to the bank on the pretext of database upgradation. The number and password are then used to carry out transactions on their behalf without their knowledge.

Phishing involves using a form of spam to fraudulently gain access to people's online banking details. As well as targeting online banking customers, phishing emails may target online auction sites or other online payment facilities. Typically, a phishing email will ask an online banking customer to follow a link in order to update personal bank account details. If the link is followed, the victim downloads a program which captures his or her banking login details and sends them to a third party.

Spam: Spam is an electronic 'junk mail' or unwanted messages sent to your email account or mobile phone. These messages vary, but are essentially commercial and often annoying in their sheer volume. They may try to persuade you to buy a product or service, or visit a website where you can make purchases; or they may attempt to trick you into divulging your bank account or credit card details.

Nigerian Scam: Nigerian or Frauds 409 or 419 are basically the lottery scam in which some overseas persons are involved to cheat innocent persons or organizations by promising to give a good amount of money at nominal fee charges. Their intention is to steal money in the form of fee against the lottery prize.

Spyware: Spyware such as Trojan Horse is generally considered to be software that is secretly installed on a computer and takes things from it without the permission or knowledge of the user. Spyware may take personal information, business information, bandwidth; or processing capacity and secretly gives it to someone else.

"Trojan Horse" scheme unfolds when malicious software (malware) embeds to a consumer's computer without the consumer being aware of it. Trojans often come in links or as attachments from unknown email senders. After installation the software detects when a person accesses online banking sites and records the username and password to transmit to the offender. People using public computers, in places like Internet cafes, are often susceptible to Trojans like malware or spyware.

Check sites URL: Always check the URL of your bank's web site. Fraudsters can lure you to enter your user ID and password at a fake website that resembles your bank. If you see anything other than the bank's genuine URL, it has to be fake.

Never enter your user ID or password or such sensitive information without ascertaining that you are on the right website. Always type the Web address of your bank into the browser address space. Never click on the link in the email.

Full-proof password: Change your online banking password at regular intervals. Also, avoid easy-to-guess passwords, like first names, birthdays, kid's or spouse's name and telephone numbers. Try to have an alpha-numeric password, one that combines alphabets and numbers.

If you have several bank accounts, never use the same online banking password for all. Never select the option on browser that stores or retains username and password. As it can easily be cracked by cyber criminals. Also, never paste your password, always type it in. This little amount of `finger exercise' will go a long way in safety.

Always check 'last logged': Most banks have a 'last logged in' panel on their websites. If your bank has it, check the panel whenever you log in. If you notice irregularities (like you are logging in after two days, but the panel says you logged in that morning!), report the matter immediately to your bank and change your password

rightaway.

Always logout when you exit the online banking portal. Close the browser to ensure that your secure session is terminated. Never exit simply by closing the browser.

Keep your system up to date: Regularly check for security updates for your computer operating system. Most security updates are aimed at reducing risks to your computer, these may be data-related or otherwise. Make sure that your operating system and browser have the latest security patches installed. And, always install these only from trusted websites.

Install a personal firewall to prevent hackers from gaining unauthorized access to your computer, especially if you connect to the Internet through a cable or a DSL modem.

Public access can be injurious: Don't leave the PC unattended after keying in information while transacting on the website. Avoid accessing your bank online at cyber cafes or on a share or public computer. Also, avoid locations that offer online connections through wireless networks (Wi-Fi), where privacy and security are minimal.

Follow Bank instructions: Banks say that appropriate upgradations are carried out from time to time by their IT departments for risk mitigation. They issue instructions to the customers to manage their accounts through virtual keyboards by way of which the characters typed by them are not identified by hackers. SMS alerts are also an important tool since any transaction carried out on account is reported to the account holder through an SMS.

Protection: Learn the ways to protect yourself from online banking fraud schemes. Detect Trojans that appear on your PC in the form of viruses, spyware or malware through Antivirus Software, anti Spyware, and Adware. Also, learn to keep your cards, documents and passwords safe, and monitor your accounts to safeguard yourself from bank fraud committed through identity theft.[60]

5.3 E-banking frauds in India

In India, the banking fraud is not so alarming compared to US and European banking sector, still it poses formidable challenge to Indian banking industry. Its effect can be felt from the fact that in the year 2004 number of cyber crime(IT act 2000 category) were 347 in India which rose to 481 in 2005 showing an increase of 38.5% while I.P.C. category crime stood at 302 in 2005 including 186 cases of cyber fraud and 68 cases cyber forgery. Thus the increasing in frauds in India is matter of concern and such frauds should be dealt with firmly. Otherwise e-banking may become a mere tool in the banking

---

[60] *ibid*

services.

In the present day global scenario, the banking system has acquired new dimensions. The banking system has entered into competitive markets in areas covering resource mobilization, human resource development, customer services and credit management. Due to these ever expanding banking services, the bank frauds have increased in last 5 years. In 2009, the Internet fraud has resulted in a loss of ` 6.6 Crores to Indian Banks from 233 reported cases. The number of credit card frauds rose from 2994 case involving ` 532 lakhs to 12959 case involving ` 3654 lakhs in 2008. It is steadily increasing According to Orissa government 83 statistics, over 13,000 credit card fraud cases were reported in India between April and December 2009. The loss of revenue stood at approximately ` 36.5 crore in 2008. A loss of ` 1147 lakhs in such transactions belonged to ICICI Bank which reported over 8280 cases.

---

[61] E- Banking, E- Payment, E- Frauds, *available at:* http://shodhganga.inflibnet.ac.in/bitstream/10603/748 01/9/chapter%203.pdf (Visited on November 1, 2017)

According to RBI, 2008 report, the number of fraud cases reported was 2658 in 2005, 2568 in 2006 and 2933 in 2007 in public sector banks in India. India's banking system has several outstanding achievements to its credit, the most striking of which is its reach. In fact, Indian banks are now spread out into the remotest areas of our country. Indian banking, which was operating in a highly comfortable and protected environment till the beginning of 1990s, has been pushed into the intense competition.

A sound banking system should possess three basic characteristics to protect depositor's interest and public faith. These are:

-Fraud free culture,

-Time tested best practice code, and

-In house immediate grievance remedial system.

All these conditions are missing or extremely weak in India.

Section 5(b) of the Banking Regulation Act, 1949 defines banking as "Banking is the accepting deposits of money for the purpose of lending or investment from the public, repayable on demand or otherwise and withdrawal by cheque, draft, order or otherwise." But if the money has fraudulently been drawn from the bank the latter is under strict obligation to pay the depositor.

The bank therefore has to ensure at all times that the money of the depositors is not drawn fraudulently. Time has come when the security aspects of the banks have to be dealt with on priority basis. The banking system in our country has been taking care of all segments of our socio-economic set up.

A bank fraud is a deliberate act of omission or commission by any person carried out in the course of banking transactions or in the books of accounts, resulting in wrongful gain to any person for a temporary period or otherwise, with or without any monetary loss to the bank.[62]

---

62 *ibid*

CHAPTER - VI
Comparative E-Banking Laws of Other Countries

In Asia, the major factor restricting growth of E-banking is security, in spite of several countries being well connected via Internet. Access to high-quality E-banking products is an issue as well. Majority of the banks in Asia are just offering basic services compared with those of developed countries. Still, E-banking seems to have a future in Asia. It is considered that E-banking will succeed if the basic features, especially bill payment, are handled well. Bill payment was the most popular feature, cited by 40 percent of respondents of the survey. However, providing this service would be difficult for banks in Asia because it requires a high level of security and involves arranging transactions with a variety of players.

The impact of E-Banking in India is not yet apparent. Many global research companies believe that E-banking adoption in India in the near future would be slow compared to other major Asian countries. Indian E-banking is still nascent, although it is fast becoming a strategic necessity for most commercial banks, as competition increases from private banks and non banking financial institutions.

6.1 United States of America

In 1995, Wells Fargo was the first U.S. bank to add account services to its website, with other banks quickly following suit. That same year, Presidential became the first U.S. bank to open bank accounts over the internet. According to research by Online Banking Report, at the end of 1999 less than 0.4% of households in the U.S. were using online banking. At the beginning of 2004, some 33 million U.S. households (31%) were using some form of online banking. Five years later, 47% of Americans used online banking, according to a survey by Gartner Group. Meanwhile, in the UK online banking grew from

63% to 70% of internet users between 2011 and 2012

By 2000, 80% of U.S. banks offered e-banking. Customer use grew slowly. At Bank of America, for example, it took 10 years to acquire 2 million e-banking customers. However, a significant cultural change took place after the Y2K scare ended. In 2001, Bank of America became the first bank to top 3 million online banking customers, more than 20% of its customer base. In comparison, larger national institutions, such as Citigroup claimed 2.2 million online relationships globally, while J.P. Morgan Chase estimated it had more than 750,000 online banking customers. Wells Fargo had 2.5 million online banking customers, including small businesses. Online customers proved more loyal and profitable than regular customers. In October 2001, Bank of America customers executed a record 3.1 million electronic bill payments, totaling more than $1 billion. In 2009, a report by Gartner Group estimated that 47% of United States adults and

30% in the United Kingdom bank online.

First online banking services in the United States

Online banking was first introduced in the early 1980s in New York, United States.[63] Four major Online banking was first introduced in the early 1980s in New York, United States.[5] Four major banks — Citibank, Chase Bank, Chemical Bank and Manufacturers Hanover — offered home banking services. Chemical introduced its Pronto services for individuals and small businesses in 1983, which enabled individual and small-business clients to maintain electronic checkbook registers, see account balances, and transfer funds between checking and savings accounts. Pronto failed to attract enough customers to break even and was abandoned in 1989. Other banks had a similar experience.

---

[63] "Banking and Finance on the Internet," edited by Mary J. Cronin

Since its inception in the United States, online banking has been federally governed by the Electronic Funds Transfer Act of 1978

6.2 United Kingdom

Almost simultaneously with the United States, online banking arrived in the United Kingdom. The UK's first home online banking services known as Homelink were set up by Bank of Scotland for customers of the Nottingham Building Society (NBS) in 1983. The system used was based on the UK's Prestel view link system and used a computer, such as the BBC Micro, or keyboard (Tandata Td1400) connected to the telephone system and television set. The system allowed on-line viewing of statements, bank transfers and bill payments. In order to make bank transfers and bill payments, a written instruction giving details of the intended recipient had to be sent to the NBS who set the details up on the Homelink system. Typical recipients were gas, electricity and telephone companies and accounts with other banks. Details of payments to be made were input into the NBS system by the account holder via Prestel. A cheque was then sent by NBS to the payee and an advice giving details of the payment was sent to the account holder. BACS was later used to transfer the payment directly.

Stanford Federal Credit Union was the first financial institution to offer online internet banking services to all of its members in October 1994. [64]

6.3 France

After a test period with 2500 users starting in 1994, online banking services were launched in 1998, using Minitel terminals that were distributed freely to the population by the government.

Eventually, 6.5 millions Minigels were installed in households in 1990. Online banking was one of the most popular services.

---

[64] Stanford Federal Credit Union Pioneers Online Financial Services

Online banking services later migrated to Internet.

The French banking industry is experiencing an increasing amount of regulation, mainly deriving from the European initiative for promoting a safe and sound banking system.

Three main layers of rules and regulations apply to banking activities:

EU law. Most of this is directly applicable in France. This includes principally the CRD IV package, which came into force under French law on 1 January 2014. This package transposes the global standards on bank capital (commonly known as the Basel III agreement) into the EU legal framework. This is achieved through Directive 2013/36/EU on capital requirements (CRD IV) and Regulation (EU) 575/2013 on prudential requirements for credit institutions and investment firms (CRR).

French legislation. Most of this is codified into the Monetary and

Financial Code (Code Monétaire et Financier). The Monetary and Financial Code has recently been amended in particular in relation to:

- The separation of banking activities, which requires the separation of own account trading activities from other activities, and imposes bans on certain other activities;
- The resolution and recovery of credit institutions;
- The regulation of payment services (which are no longer part of the French banking monopoly rules), electronic currencies and FinTech. In a addition: Ordinance of 23 June 2016 implemented Directive 2014/65/EU on markets in financial instruments (MiFID II), in respect of automated and algorithmic negotiation, inducements, distribution of financial instruments and investment advisory activities; Ordinance of 1 December 2016 reinforced money laundering rules;

- Law of 9 December 2016 (Loi Sapin 2) principally oriented towards fighting against corruption extended the whistleblower activities in the financial sector to any non-complying behavior and not only to market abuse.

Regulatory authority regulations.

Detailed regulations enacted by regulatory authorities like the European Central Bank (ECB), the Prudential and Resolution Control Authority (Autorité de Contrôle Prudentiel et de Résolution) (ACPR) or the French Financial Market Authority (Autorité des marchés financiers) (AMF).

_____

_____

CHAPTER - VII
Implication for Improving
E-banking System

India continues to be a unique market and regulatory environment with intense involvement of the regulator and the government. Hopefully, the rapid outreach will make the model sustainable for all banks and at the same time offer services really needed by the clients. These two ends are, of course, aligned and mutually beneficial.

E-banking is changing the banking industry and is causing major effects on banking relationships and its working nature. E-banking involves use of internet for delivery of banking products and services. Advantages previously held by large financial institutions have shrunk considerably. The internet has leveled the playing field and afforded open access to customers in the global marketplace. E-banking is a cost effective delivery channel for financial institutions. Consumers are embracing many benefits of E-banking. Access to one's account at anytime and from anywhere via World Wide Web is a convenient style. Thus, a bank's internet presence transforms from 'brochureware' status to 'E-banking' status once the bank goes through a technology integration plan which enables the customer to access information about his or her specific account relationship.

The six primary drivers of e banking includes, in order of primacy are:

1. Improve customer access.

2. Facilitate the offering of more services.

3. Attract new customers.

4. Provide services offered by competitors.

5. Reduce customer attrition.

A multi-layered security architecture comprising firewalls, filtering routers, encryption and digital certification ensures that customers account information is protected from unauthorized access. Apart from this, the Reserve Bank of India has issued circular for the convenience of working with electronic banking as there is a steep rise in internet banking.

The need of the hour is to meet the global challenge of providing different services to customers and also keeping vigil eye, to curtail the risk arising due to E-banking. In the light of above discussion over the matter, the researcher warrants to make certain suggestions-

1. Banks are under obligation to maintain secrecy of customer's account. The new RBI circular has given guidelines to minimize risk of hacking. However, it is the duty on the banker to adopt technology to discharge his duty in a more effective manner. Reserve Bank of India should also ensure that the banks are using new technology. The RBI should appoint technicians and ask them to report the same under security policy.

2. The auditor appointed to inform as the misappropriation of funds even at the minutest level. Electronic banking has enhanced the risk of misappropriation of funds by the bankers as it goes undetected.

3. The Automatic Teller Machine is widely used today. It is observed that these machines fail frequently and causes inconvenience to the customer. RBI in its next circular has to mention the number of times banks are not penalized for such failures. After a particular limit the banks should pay penalty which alerts them to keep check on the working of the machine. Speedier and cheaper justice is the hallmark of the Consumer Protection Act and as discussed above the Act is application to banking service also. The scope of the Act should be extended specifically to electronic banking also in cases of frequent failure of ATM machines, non compliance of security which results in hacking, and exuberant charges levied by bank for fund transfer, etc. Though these are covered under RBI circular, they should be brought within the

purview of the legislation, which will be convenient to customers.

The gradual regulatory evolution to support banks in their outreach efforts continues and the results are beginning to emerge. Increasing competition has become a challenge for Indian banks but it also provides thoughtful opportunities to develop the banking business as per international standards. The technology holds the key to success of Indian banks as India could leapfrog into internet banking. Customers of Indian banks are still reluctant in adopting electronic banking. Understanding the reasons for this resistance would be useful for bank managers in formulating strategies aimed at increasing online banking use. Crime based on electronic offences are bound to increase and the law makers have to go the extra mile compared to the fraudsters, to keep them at bay. Technology is always a double-edged sword and can be used for both the purposes, good or bad.

Preamble of the IT Act 2000 provides that the Act was passed with the objective to give legal recognition for transactions carried out by means of electronic data interchange and other means of e-commerce. Further the Act has also made amendments to the IPC 1860, Indian Evidence Act 1872, The Bankers Books of Evidence Act 1891, and the Reserve Bank of India Act 1934 for facilitating legal recognition and regulation of the commercial activities.

Though this objective of the Act is not to suppress the commercial activity, but has defined certain offences and penalties to smother such omissions, which is understood to come within the characterization of cyber crimes. For customers security is still a big concern for usage of e-banking services which the present legislation is inadequate to deal with. The challenges ahead to the court of law to apply the provisions have been difficult due to lack of clarity.

With the time, the concept of internet banking has got attention in the Indian context. Most of the banks have already implemented the e-banking facilities, as these facilities are beneficial to both i.e. banks as well as consumers. But the adoption of e-banking by the consumers is still at the early stage due to various challenges. The challenges such as security risk, privacy risk, trust factor and less awareness among consumers about e-banking are acting as hurdle in the adoption of e-banking facilities. Considering the challenges and risk related to e-banking, the Government of India along with various government agencies is making an effort to make e-banking more safe, secure and reliable. The paper only presents the overview of Internet banking in Indian context. Studies in the past have shown that with the time Indian consumers are opting internet banking services with the time. Considering this in mind, the future studies may be conducted to analyze the various factors which influence the consumer intention to adopt internet banking services.

Internet banking is a popular and convenient method of doing online banking transactions. We have no dedicated Internet banking laws in India but the Reserve Bank of India (RBI) has issued some guidelines in this regard. However, Internet banking guidelines in India by RBI are not sufficient to make the banks follow robust and required cyber security procedures.

This means that Internet banking risks in India are high and even RBI acknowledged risks of e-banking in India. Despite this position, banks in India are ignoring the cyber security due diligence requirements prescribed by RBI. The online banking risks in India have increased tremendously due to this position. RBI has also released a report of the RBI working group on securing card present transaction in order to provide preventive measures for ATM frauds in India. Sill Internet banking frauds in India and ATM Frauds are increasing.

Banks in India are not serious about cyber security and they are not following the recommendations of RBI.

RBI has also insisted upon ensuring of cyber security of banks in India. In fact, recently RBI warned Indian banks for inadequate cyber security as well. This is resulting in increased financial crimes and cyber crimes in India. Mobile banking cyber security in India is also at risk. The legal issues of Internet banking in India must be taken more seriously by all stakeholders especially the Indian banks. However, better results cannot be achieved till cyber security requirements made mandatory on the part of Indian banks. The way a country regulates its financial and banking sectors is in some senses a snapshot of its priorities, its goals, and the type of financial landscape and society it would like to engineer. In the case of India, the regulations passed by its reserve bank give us a glimpse into its approaches to financial governance and shows the degree to which it prioritizes stability within its banking sector, as well as economic inclusiveness.

Regulatory framework in India has gone a long way forward, with the Information Technology Act 2000 attempting to address a number of e-commerce regulatory issues, address the need for banks to go online and have laid out security measures to be adopted (since online baking is overlapping with e-commerce on most occasions and having to deal with cross-border jurisdictions), and with the comprehensive and forward looking guidelines brought out by the RBI.

Along with the favorable scenario in the techno-legal aspect and the increasing internet consumer base has taken the trend of online banking from basic information dissemination service to fund-based transactions on their accounts, hinting at the ample growth prospect of online banking in India in the Internet banking system, information is considered as an asset and so worthy of protection. However, the present system of authentication does not address the security aspect in full. This calls for an urgent need to acclimatize the whole system. According to Online Banking Association, member institutions rated security as the most important issue of online banking. There is a dual requirement to protect customers' privacy and protection against fraud. Another major issue is that of Data Protection and the need for a legal and regulatory framework. Currently, India has no law on data protection. Information security in e-banking present's two main areas of risk: preventing unauthorized transactions and maintaining integrity of customers' transactions. Data protection falls in the latter. Data protection laws primarily aim to safeguard the interest of the individual whose data is handled and processed by others. 'Interests' are usually expressed in terms of privacy, autonomy and/or integrity. The Information Technology Act, 2000 does not address this issue. India should take cue from nations, which have favored ad hoc enactment of sectoral laws over omnibus legislation. Along with these issues, the contradictory issues present in the Banking Regulations Act, 1949, the Reserve Bank of India Act, 1934 and the Foreign Exchange Management Act, 1999 need also to be looked into. On the technological front the Indian Internet banking system is facing many hurdles. The problems include operational risks, security risks, system architecture risks, reputational risks and legal risks. Phishing is another issue that needs attention. Experts suggest that simple rules such as not sharing login IDs and passwords

with anyone, would keep customers
safe.

BIBLIOGRAPHY

Statutes

- Banking Regulation Act,1949
- Information Technology Act, 2000
- Indian Contract Act,1872
- Indian Penal Code,1806
- Securities Contracts(Regulations) Act,1956

Books

- *Private Equity Law and Practice by* Darryl J Cooke, Sweet Maxwell South Asian Edition, 4th Edition, 2013
- *Supreme Court on Banking Law by* S.N Gupta, Universal Law Publishing Co., 5th Edition, 2007
- *Ellinger's Modern Banking Law by* E.P Ellinger and R.J.A Hoole, Oxford

University, 1st Indian Edition, 4th International Edition,2007

- *CPC by* Mulla Lexis Nexis Butterworths Wadhwa, 18th Edition,2011,Vol. 2,2011
- *Banking Theory Law and Practice by* Sundaram and P.N Varshney, Sultan Chand & Sons,2013
- *Paget's Laws on Banking by* Mark Hapgood Q.C, Lexis and Nexis Butterwoods, 13th Edition, March 2007
- *Practical System of Book Keeping "By Double and Single Entry", Oliver L Briggs* by Benjamin Wood Foster, 17th Edition
- *Foreclosure of Hypothecation by* John S Nightingale, Govt. Press, 1845
- *A correspondence Relating to Hypothecation of 500 Bonds by* James

Van, Worden and Co., Pine street, 1842

- *The Law and Practice of International Finance Series by* Philips R. Wood, Vol. 2,2[nd] Edition, Thomson Sweet and Maxwell
- *History of Money and Banking in U.S by* Murray N. Rothbard, Ludwig Von Mises Institute,2002
- *History of Banking by* William John Lawson, Stanford University Library,1850, London
- *Development of Banking in India by* Dr.Kushal K. Arora, Atlantic Publisher and Distributor
- *Modern Banking in India by* K.C Sharma, Deep and Deep Publications Pvt. Ltd. , 2007

- *World Bank History by* Dinesh Kapoor, Brooking Institution Press, Vol. 1 , 1997
- *Strategic Credit Management in Banks by* G.S. Popli and S.K Puri, P.H.I Learning Pvt. Ltd. , 2012
- *Elements of Banking and Insurance* by Jyotsna Sethi and Nishwan Bhatia, 2nd Edition, P.H.I Learning Pvt. Ltd. , 2013
- *Legal and Regulatory Aspects of Banking by* Macmillan, Indian Institute of Banking and Finance, 2nd Edition, 2010
- *Management of Banking and Financial Services by* Suresh Padmalatha, Pearson Publishing House, 2nd Edition, 2010

Journals

- Adverse Selection Market Access and Intermarket Competition by Peter Hoffman, Vol. 65, April 2016, p.g 108 – 119

- Credit Market Sentiments and Business Cycle by David Lopez Salido, January 2016, NBER WORKING PAPER SERIES No. 21879

- What are the factors that are affecting public sector banks by Denedra Jain

- An Empirical Study of Joint Production and Scale Economies in Commercial Banking by Thomas W Gilligan and Michael L Smirlock, Vol. 8, Issue 1, March 1984, p.g 67 – 77

- Enforcement of Securities Interest in Banking Transaction by Rashmi Grover and Anish Banga,

Survey_summary_India (2) (1).pdf enforcement main.pdf Juris Corp Advocates in Solicitors

Websites

- www.yourliberary.com
- www.bankingawarness.com
- www.co-operative.com
- www.gktoday.com
- www.academia.com
- www.bizfinance.about.com
- www.investopedia.com
- www.karpuramanjari.blogspot

NEWSPAPERS ARTICLES

The Economics Times

_____

_____

_____

www.ingramcontent.com/pod-product-compliance
Lightning Source LLC
Chambersburg PA
CBHW071448220526
45472CB00003B/722